1 Altruism and Aggression: What Are They?

> KEY AIMS: By the end of Part 1 you will:
> ➤ *know what psychologists mean by altruism and aggression;*
> ➤ *be aware of the ways in which we can ethically study altruism and aggression;*
> ➤ *understand that social psychology is only one of many levels of explanation that can be offered.*

A woman is walking home past her local primary school when she sees two older boys surrounding a little boy. Their mocking laughter turns into pushing and fighting. She orders the boys to stop but they ignore her. She tries to pull them away but they resist her. In desperation she grabs one of the older boys and slaps him. The little boy runs away to safety. Did her prosocial aims justify her antisocial acts?

Figure 1.1: Children fighting

A man enters a blood transfusion centre and donates blood. Two weeks later he is diagnosed as suffering from AIDS. The blood he has given has been passed on to many others who risk developing the same illness. Did his prosocial aim excuse the antisocial consequences? These examples indicate some of the problems in defining what we mean by the terms **prosocial** and **antisocial**.

Prosocial behaviour and altruism

Prosocial behaviour is a large category which includes actions designed to benefit others or to have positive social consequences. It might include standing for parliament, becoming a doctor, or donating to charity. In social psychology, altruism has been the main focus of study. An **altruistic** act is defined as an act that benefits someone else when there is no expectation of reward to the actor. This seems straightforward, but can this ever be true? When you help a woman who has dropped her shopping in the street, don't you feel the benefit of a heightened sense of self-esteem? When you ignore a homeless person in the street but later put money in a collecting can for a charity which helps the homeless, don't you feel a reduction in guilt? When you help a classmate with their homework, don't you expect that the favour will be returned at a later date? There are many invisible rewards for altruism which we shall examine later.

Our definition of altruism does help to rule out some areas of prosocial behaviour – we exclude nurses and doctors because they receive direct rewards (a salary) for their acts. Our definition also distinguishes altruism from *co-operation* – joint action where both parties immediately benefit from working together. You and your friend may decide to help each other revise for the psychology exam that you will both be taking, but you are not being altruistic – both of you get a direct pay-off. What if you selflessly agree to test your friend on her economics revision and at a later date she spontaneously offers to help you with your psychology? Where one person acts altruistically and then is repaid at a later date, we call it *delayed reciprocal altruism*. Some people argue that this form of exchange is the very basis of human relationships and society (Ridley, 1996).

SAQ
1

Is *altruism one form of prosocial behaviour, or is prosocial behaviour one form of altruism?*

Anti-social behaviour and aggression

Antisocial behaviour includes acts which cause harm to others. This might include theft, burglary, fraud and deception, in addition to outright physical injury. Although we shall briefly consider these forms of social and economic 'cheating' in the next chapter, we will focus mainly on aggression. **Aggression** is usually defined as an intended injurious act that the victim is motivated to avoid.

We have to refer to intention so that we can rule out acts which were unforeseen. If I throw open a door which you happen to be standing behind and break your nose in the process, we might consider my

behaviour careless, but hardly aggressive. The football pitch is one place where the element of intention is crucial to deciding whether a foul has been committed or not. The referee has to infer an aggressive intention from the person's actions, and it is no wonder some mistakes are made.

We also need to include the idea of an unwilling victim in order to rule out acts which cause harm, but which the victim wants. For example, an appendectomy involves a degree of intended injury on the part of the surgeon (cutting someone's body open), but the patient has agreed to the procedure.

Figure 1.2: A football foul

Sado-masochistic encounters between consenting adults involve agreement by the victim and so under this definition would not be aggressive. (However, in 1997 the European Court refused to recognize the argument that victim assent made the act non-criminal.)

Most researchers reserve the term *violence* for physical forms of aggression causing significant bodily injury that renders the act liable to criminal sanction.

CONTENTS

PART 1: ALTRUISM AND AGGRESSION: WHAT ARE THEY? 1
Prosocial behaviour and altruism 1
Anti-social behaviour and aggression 2
    What aggression is not 3
Carrying out research on altruism and aggression 3
    Experiments 3
    Field studies 4
    Questionnaires 4
    Criminological studies 6
Levels of explanation 7

PART 2: ALTRUISM AND RELATIONSHIPS 9
Altruism as an evolutionary problem 9
    Kin selection 9
    Reciprocal altruism 10
    Do humans show kin and reciprocal altruism? 11
Exchange relationships 13
Communal relationships 15

PART 3: ALTRUISM AND EMOTIONS 17
Empathy and distress 17
The effects of prior mood 20
Costs of being helped: Status and help-seeking 22
Costs of helping: Bystander apathy 23
    Interpretation 23
    Audience inhibition 24
    Diffusion of responsibility 24

PART 4: INSTRUMENTAL THEORIES OF AGGRESSION 25
Evolutionary functions of instrumental aggression 25
Social learning theory 27
    What are the payoffs for aggression? 28
Cognitive social learning theory 31
    Hostile attributional bias 32
Reducing aggression 33

PART 5: EXPRESSIVE THEORIES OF AGGRESSION 34
Evolutionary functions of expressive aggression 34
Psychoanalytic theory 34
Frustration—aggression theory 35
Cognitive Neo-Associationist Theory 37
Arousal Transfer Theory 40
Reducing aggression 41

PART 6: THE IMPACT OF CULTURE 43
What is culture? 43
The medium of social transmission 44
    Theories of the television—violence relationship 44
    Viewing television violence and behaviour 45
The Cultural Message 47
    Values 47
    Interpretations 48
Summing up 51

REFERENCES 52

FURTHER READING 53

ANSWERS TO SELF-ASSESSMENT QUESTIONS 54

GLOSSARY 56

ACKNOWLEDGEMENTS 58

Physical aggression is sometimes used as a synonym for violence but usually refers to acts of physical assault where the injury is less serious. *Verbal aggression* is used to describe episodes of verbal attack and abuse. Recent research has examined *indirect aggression* – acts in which there is no direct confrontation with the victim and the attacker seeks to conceal their identity (Bjorkqvist, Osterman and Lagerspetz, 1994). Examples would include attacking someone's character behind their back and getting other people to ignore the victim or exclude them from activities.

Does gossiping about others really count as an act of aggression?

What aggression is not

Just as important as the question of what aggression is, is what it is *not*. Aggression is *not anger* – this is an emotion which may or may not accompany aggression. We often experience anger without showing it, especially when the target is in a position of authority over us, such as a teacher, employer or parent. On the other hand, when a Mafia hitman executes a business rival there may be no element of anger whatever. Aggression is *not hostility* – we may experience generalized hostility ('Everyone is out to get me'), or specific hostility ('I can't stand my next-door-neighbour'), without expressing it in aggressive acts. Aggression is not *ambitiousness* or *high achievement motivation*. Although we speak of 'aggressive salesmen', we do not seriously mean that they beat up or verbally abuse their prospective clients. Aggression is *not competition*. Wanting to out-do another person in a sports event or an exam does not usually involve any attempt to harm them.

What differences exist between ambition, aggression, anger and hostility?

A POSSIBLE PROJECT

Buy the same newspaper for a week. (If possible, have your friends also buy a paper each, but a different one.) Define carefully what you will count as antisocial and prosocial behaviour. Decide whether you are going to include political stories (MPs debate new Criminal Justice Bill) as well as human interest stories ('Boy saves granny'). For the first five pages of each edition, count up the total number of stories and then the number that describe antisocial behaviour and the number that describe prosocial behaviour. Which type of behaviour gets reported more? Why do you think that might be? Which newspaper reports the most antisocial events?

Carrying out research on altruism and aggression

Once we have defined what we mean by aggression and altruism, we need to consider the next step – how can we measure them in our research?

Experiments

Aggression has been especially problematic for researchers because of the ethical prohibition on harming participants – we cannot create situations in which people actually injure another person either physically or psychologically. One experimental technique that has often been used in the United States is the administration of electric shocks. Participants are told that they will take part in a reaction-time competition against an opponent. Whoever loses the contest will be given a shock by their opponent. The participants are allowed to see the level of shock that has been selected for them by their opponent (who is actually a confederate of the researcher) and are then asked to decide what level of shock *they* wish to give if they win. The higher the shock they select, the more aggressively they are behaving. In other studies, participants are insulted by the experimenter and then asked to make a written evaluation of his or her competence.

The major problem with such experiments is their obvious artificiality. We do not usually express aggression by giving electric shocks or writing negative evaluations and we do not do it in a laboratory under the eye of a researcher who takes moral responsibility for our behaviour. In experiments we are dealing with a stranger whom we will never meet again, whereas most real-world aggression occurs between people who know one another. We are also unlikely to be retaliated against in the laboratory so our normal level of fear and restraint may be lower.

Researchers into altruism have also used experimental techniques, but are less affected by ethical problems. (They are not entirely free of them, however. Participants may be distressed when they learn after the experiment that, while others helped, they behaved selfishly.) Typically, a situation is created where, after some experimental manipulation, the participant has a choice about helping another person. They may be asked to donate blood, or give up their experimental payment to charity, or get help for someone who appears to be ill.

Field studies

Altruism and aggression can also be studied in the field. Experimenters have gone onto New York subway trains and pretended to faint. It was found that being dressed like a tramp and smelling of alcohol affects how much help people give. Researchers who study aggression have sent out confederates to stall their cars at green traffic lights and report the amount of horn-honking by other motorists. Others have cut into queues at supermarket checkouts to examine the reactions of waiting shoppers. Another technique is to simply wait for aggression or altruism to occur spontaneously and then observe it. Observational studies of real-world aggression are difficult because public aggression is rare and unpredictable. In the area of altruism, some researchers have taken advantage of real life emergencies to examine the motives and personalities of those who risk their life to save others.

Questionnaires

Researchers use questionnaires to ask about participants' responses to imaginary situations or to report on episodes of altruism or aggression in which they have been involved. Others use standardized psychometric inventories to measure aggression or altruism as traits (see Box 1.1). This trait approach assumes that there is a generalized tendency within each individual to behave altruistically or aggressively, which is stable over time and across different situations (Olweus, 1979). The psychometric inventories are composed of many items designed to sample a wide domain of behaviours, preferences or beliefs which are summed to give an overall score. They are developed on a large sample of people and once their validity has been established, these measures of altruism and aggression can be correlated with other variables.

Box 1.1: Some items from *The Aggression Questionnaire*. This questionnaire was designed by Arnold Buss and Mark Perry in 1992. It measures four components – *physical aggression, verbal aggression, anger* and *hostility*. Participants are asked to endorse the extent to which each statement is true for them.

Once in a while I get the urge to strike another person.

Extremely uncharacteristic of me ___ ___ ___ ___ ___ Extremely characteristic of me

I tell my friends openly when I disagree with them.

Extremely uncharacteristic of me ___ ___ ___ ___ ___ Extremely characteristic of me

I flare up quickly but get over it quickly.

Extremely uncharacteristic of me ___ ___ ___ ___ ___ Extremely characteristic of me

I am sometimes eaten up with jealousy.

Extremely uncharacteristic of me ___ ___ ___ ___ ___ Extremely characteristic of me

Given enough provocation, I may hit another person.

Extremely uncharacteristic of me ___ ___ ___ ___ ___ Extremely characteristic of me

I often find myself disagreeing with people.

Extremely uncharacteristic of me ___ ___ ___ ___ ___ Extremely characteristic of me

When frustrated I let my irritation show.

Extremely uncharacteristic of me ___ ___ ___ ___ ___ Extremely characteristic of me

At times I feel I have gotten a raw deal out of life.

Extremely uncharacteristic of me ___ ___ ___ ___ ___ Extremely characteristic of me

SOMETHING TO TRY

How useful for psychology are personal recollections and accounts? Ask a friend about a time they behaved altruistically or aggressively. How do they describe the event? What motives do they attribute to themselves? Do altruists try to downplay their acts, and if so, why? Do aggressors try to justify their acts, and if so, why? (See Box 1.2)

Box 1.2: *Violent individuals talking about their lives can provide a rich source of information on an insider's perspective on motivations and techniques. The following section is from the autobiography of John Allen, a street criminal.*

Robbing is an art and the whole art of robbing is fear, and the main reason for robbing is to get what you came after – the money – and get away. You don't go in there to hurt people. Sometimes you have to. Sometimes you do it in self-defense or because the person is trying to protect their property, but most of the time that somebody gets hurt is when somebody bucks, 'I'm not giving you nothing. If you want it, you'll have to kill me'. I heard that a lot of times, but you don't really have to do that. If you instil fear the moment the robbery started to take place, then you got more than half the battle won. When you succeed in getting away – find a good escape route – then that's the whole battle right there.

Occasionally somebody say, 'I ain't giving up nothing.' But you can change his tune easy. You ain't got to kill him. Smack him with the gun or shoot him in the foot or the kneecap, he give it right up. Knock his big toe off with one of them .45s, he give it up. I think it's probably my background that it don't bother me.

When I was a kid, before I really got into the stickup thing, my family kind of had other hopes for me and sometimes so did I. For a while I thought about going into the Navy to see the world. My grandmother, she wanted me to be a doctor because I was good with my hands. And my mother she wanted me to be a lawyer. Maybe it could have come to pass, but I really couldn't see it because that meant working real hard in school. I asked somebody about being a doctor, I think it was one of the playground dudes who ran little recreation things. And they was saying you got to go here for three years and do this for three years and do this for three more years. Before I could be a doctor, I'd be withered away.

People constantly saying, 'Why don't you do better? Why don't you do this or do that?' I don't know how to do this. I don't know how to do that. This is all I know. I know how to steal. I know how to be hard on broads. I know how to stick somebody up better than anything. I know how to take a small piece of narcotics and eventually work it way up and make some money. Fencing property or credit cards, I know how to do all that. But society says all that's wrong. I feel like it's survival, making the dollar. I don't have nothing against a guy that makes a dollar. Whatever his bag is, that's his bag.

(Taken from John Allen (1978). *Assault with a Deadly Weapon: The Autobiography of a Street Criminal*. New York: McGraw Hill.)

Criminological studies

Crime rates obtained from police and courts can be examined and compared across age, sex, historical periods or nations. However, many crimes, such as marital assaults, child abuse and school bullying are often not reported to the police and, even when they are, no arrest may be made. We cannot be sure how much crime statistics reflect differences in police efficiency (clear-up rate) or practice (use of cautioning). To avoid this problem, some researchers use self-report crime questionnaires where people are asked to report anonymously the kinds of crimes they have committed. We can also employ victimization surveys such as the British Crime Survey, where a representative sample of people are asked to describe the offences of which they have been a victim. We presume that people are more willing to report being a victim than being an offender, and these data allow estimates of the actual amount of crime taking place, whether or not it is reported to the police.

What data sources can social scientists use to find out about anti-social behaviour?

A POSSIBLE PROJECT

At your local library, try to get hold of the Criminal Statistics for the UK issued each year by the Home Office. Is there more violent crime or more property crime? What percentage of offenders are male? Which age group commits the most crime? How does your local reporting district compare with its neighbours?

Levels of explanation

Many disciplines have been interested in altruism and aggression. To put social psychology in context, Box 1.3 indicates some of the different levels of explanation that can be offered.

Evolutionary theory looks at how natural and sexual selection would have favoured individuals who displayed different levels of altruism and aggression in the environment of human adaptation about 200,000 years ago. We shall discuss this in more detail later.

These selection pressures have resulted in the particular gene pool around us today. *Behaviour genetics* is interested in determining the extent to which current individual differences in altruism and aggression have a genetic basis. By studying identical and non-identical twins (either living together or separated at birth), and by studying adopted children, behaviour geneticists are able to estimate the power of genes to explain differences between people. Genetic factors explain approximately 51 per cent of the differences in levels of altruism that exist between people, and about 39 per cent of the differences in aggression (Rushton *et al.*, 1986).

Neuroanatomical and *neurochemical* researchers try to identify the parts of the brain that are responsible for different behaviours and to identify the chemical transmitters that relay messages to and from the appropriate centres. The *hypothalamus* is involved in the regulation of aggression and the *preoptic area* has recently been found to show sex differences in line with the universal finding of higher levels of aggression among males. In addition, the *neurotransmitter serotonin* is lower in males and has recently been implicated in the control of aggression.

Developmental studies look at the typical pattern of development of altruism and aggression and at the environmental factors (such as parenting practices, peers, siblings and intervention strategies) that increase or decrease levels of the target behaviour.

Trait theorists view aggression and altruism as enduring dispositions that characterize an individual. They develop and employ questionnaires to assess these traits and to examine their stability over time and situations. Often they see if one trait (such as **empathy**) is related to another (altruism).

Social psychologists are especially interested in the social *context* and *situations* in which altruism and aggression appear. Communities may or may not tolerate aggression or expect altruism from their members. They may expect different

Box 1.3: Levels of explanation adopted by psychologists who study prosocial and antisocial behaviour.

LEVEL OF EXPLANATION	CONCERNED WITH	TYPICAL QUESTIONS
Evolutionary	Differential reproductive success in the environment of evolutionary adaptation.	How and why did altruism and aggression benefit individuals?
Behaviour Genetic	Explanatory power of genes and environment in contemporary populations.	How do predispositions interact with unique learning experiences?
Neurological	Neuroanatomical and neurochemical regulation of behaviour.	Which parts of the brain and which neuro-transmitters are involved in altruism and aggression?
Developmental	Factors affecting the development of competencies and behaviour in children.	Does television viewing affect children's levels of altruism or aggression?
Trait	Differences between individuals that are stable over time and situations.	Are women less aggressive than men?
Cultural	Values and norms which promote or depress behaviours.	Do cultures vary in the extent to which they encourage and reward altruism and aggression?
Situational	Immediate environmental triggers which promote or inhibit behaviours.	Does the presence of others increase altruism and aggression?

amounts from adults than from children, or from one sex than the other. These commonly-held expectations are called *norms*. *Situational analysis* is also very common in social psychology studies. By changing aspects of the situation (as independent variables) we see how the target behaviour (dependent variable) changes. We can examine how, for example, altruism increases or decreases in response to the number of potential helpers, the degree of apparent need, or the cost of helping. Sometimes we are interested in how this situational information is attended to and processed. *Attribution theory* studies whether the causes we attribute to another's behaviour ('It's their own fault – they brought it on themselves') affect the likelihood of altruism or aggression. We can see that social psychology is one of many levels of explanation, and that social scientists must attempt to unite their research findings to build a comprehensive model of human altruism and aggression.

Altruism and Relationships

KEY AIMS: By the end of Part 2 you will:
- ➤ recognize a distinction between kin and reciprocal altruism in animals;
- ➤ see that communal and exchange relationships form a parallel system in humans;
- ➤ understand that social norms actively promote altruism.

Altruism as an evolutionary problem

Altruism posed a major problem for Darwin's theory of **natural selection**. Darwin believed that those individuals most adapted to their environment would survive better and reproduce more prolifically than others, and their offspring (also possessing these 'fit' characteristics) would be represented in the next generation more numerously.

Imagine a situation at the dawn of our species *Homo sapiens*, about 200,000 years ago. A predator stealthily approaches a group of young women. One woman notices its approach and gives an alarm call to the others, pointing to the danger. The others have time to hide, but by drawing attention to herself, the woman is killed. Her altruism has led to her own death and to that of her future children who would have also behaved altruistically. If she had kept quiet and hidden without giving a warning, the predator would have eaten someone else. Darwin concluded that altruism was not a 'fit' strategy, since it led to greater vulnerability than did a strategy of selfishness. He suspected it would be the logical downfall of his theory.

Kin selection

Darwin, however, knew little of the mechanics of genetics. We now know that during fertilization, the zygote receives half its **genes** from the mother and half from the father. When that child grows up and reproduces, it will supply half the genes of its own offspring, half of which will have come from its own mother. So one quarter of a grandchild's full complement of genes will have come from its grandmother. These figures are an index of genetic relatedness. If the unit of selection is

Figure 2.1: Photo of mother and baby

not the individual but the gene, then by saving someone who is related to us we have in essence saved a part of ourselves. J.B.S. Haldane, a famous biochemist and geneticist, reputedly said that he would be prepared to sacrifice his life for two brothers or eight cousins. This is the basis of **kin selection**, and depends upon understanding that our fitness is not measured only by our own survival and reproduction, but also by the survival and reproduction of all those who carry our genes. Thus a gene for altruism could survive and be passed on if it lived in the bodies of the relatives of the woman who gave warning of the approach of the predator and was eaten. Note that kin selection derives from people being 'in the same boat', genetically speaking. Your personal success is intimately tied to your kin's success. We will meet this idea again in the form of what social psychologists call **communal relationships**.

Identical twins share all their genes while non-identical twins share only half. Which type of twins should show the most altruism to one another?

Reciprocal altruism

However, we behave altruistically not only to kin, but also to friends and acquaintances – sometimes even to strangers. This form of altruism is called **reciprocal altruism** and depends on a 'You scratch my back and I'll scratch yours' principle. Because there is often a delay between the altruistic act and the reciprocation of the act, it occurs in those species where members live in stable social groups, have long memories, and a good ability to recognize and distinguish faces.

Imagine that you and I are in the same social group of early hominids. I find a huge patch of wild berries but I have just eaten a full meal. You are literally starving and near death. Should I give them to you? Under reciprocal altruism there are four important factors:

Figure 2.2: A chimp begging food

1 The cost of helping – in this case the costs are low since I am too full to eat them anyway. Had I been starving too, I would have been less generous.

2 The likely future benefits accruing to me. In this case, they are very high because I have literally saved your life. You will then have an obligation to repay me at a very high level.

3 The probability that I will need help in the future. If we are living under risky conditions, where we may face famine or drought or injury, then I may well need help from others sooner or later.

4 The probability that you would reciprocate. Here I must rely on your past record of reciprocating help and, if I do not have first-hand experience, I may have to rely on your reputation in the community.

Note that these considerations imply a form of *cost-benefit analysis* – we shall meet this idea again in the form of social psychologists' notion of *equity* theory.

To behave altruistically does not require that we calculate the past history and future probability of repayment, just as to catch a ball accurately we do not have to know the physical laws that determine trajectory and velocity. Instead of mathematical calculations, emotions can act as signals for whether we owe or are owed by others. Robert Trivers (1985) has suggested that warmth and pride are associated with helping others; guilt is associated with our failure to repay an act of kindness; obligation is an emotion which calibrates the amount we owe to another in future; and anger and desire for punishment tell us that someone we have helped has no intention of repaying their debt.

SAQ
5

What three capacities does a species need to have to make reciprocal altruism an effective strategy?

SOMETHING TO TRY

Ask some of your friends when they last felt guilty. Do their replies support Trivers' idea about the origin of guilt?

Do humans show kin and reciprocal altruism?

Most evolutionary psychologists believe that reciprocal altruism evolved out of kin altruism. One suggestion is that the warm feelings associated with reciprocal altruism are similar to those we feel for our genetic relatives and this sense of love or empathy prompts us to help friends also. Another suggestion is that we help others who share genes similar to our own and if their past altruistic behaviour suggests that they carry altruistic genes like us, we help them to survive and propagate as we would our own genetic relatives.

The point is that kin and reciprocal altruism in humans may be two ends of the same continuum rather than two distinct strategies. This point is clear when we consider husbands and wives. They share no genes, but engage in a degree of mutual altruism so high as to suggest they effectively feel as close as kin. (They also frequently share a heavy investment in the survival of their joint progeny to whom both are related.) There are probably individual differences in

Box 2.1: Are women more communal than men?

We have used the terms communal and exchange to describe two kinds of relationships. But people may vary in whether they interpret relationships as communal- or exchange-based. In 1974, two researchers working independently, Sandra Bem (1974) and Janet Spence (Spence, Helmreich and Stapp, 1974), developed psychometric scales which they called *masculinity* and *femininity*. The two researchers produced scales which are highly correlated and very similar. The femininity scale measures the extent to which people describe themselves as 'warm', 'caring', 'dependent' and 'nurturing'. The masculinity scale measures how highly people rate themselves with adjectives such as 'competitive', 'independent' and 'strong under pressure'. Although these adjectives were initially derived from ratings of male and female stereotypes, when participants were directly asked to rate themselves, consistent sex differences appeared in dozens of studies. Janet Spence believes we should not call these scales 'masculinity' and 'femininity' but rather 'agency' and 'communion'. She believes they are measures of interpersonal orientation, and, although they are correlated with gender, they do not themselves constitute gender. Women appear as consistently more communal than men. This finding was replicated in a different study by Alan Feingold (1994), using people from many nations. He took advantage of the fact that when psychologists develop personality tests they are required to collect data from many hundreds of people to validate them. He compared men's and women's scores on a variety of traits and found that women exceed men on anxiety, trust, tender-mindedness and gregariousness, while men exceed women on assertiveness.

It may be that women tend to view their relationships in more communal terms – that is, in terms of responding to others' needs while men tend to view them more as an exchange relationship in which help given today can be repaid at a later date. Carol Gilligan (1982) has worked on the way that men and women solve interpersonal dilemmas. She has argued that women focus upon meeting each party's needs and maintaining good relations, while men tend to focus upon achieving justice even at the expense of a relationship. We know too that men's mental health is improved by marriage while women's suffers. Perhaps women's responsiveness to others' needs leads to a greater psychological burden than men typically carry.

people's tendency to view relationships in these two terms, and women seem to see others more in terms of 'kin feelings' than do men.

Why might women view relationships in more communal terms than men do?

Because most social psychologists have favoured laboratory or field experiments, they have generally examined altruism toward strangers or abstract charitable causes. Evolutionary psychology leads us to expect that helping strangers would be governed by reciprocal altruism, while helping relatives and intimates might look more like kin altruism. Margaret Clark (1984;1989) has focused on the distinction between partners and strangers in her work and refers to these two forms of altruism as **communal** and **exchange** relations. For simplicity I have split these two forms in *Box 2.2*, but they are better seen as a continuum running from kin altruism (communal relations) to reciprocal altruism (exchange relations). This continuum corresponds to the order in which people help in the aftermath of natural disasters; first we help family members, then friends and neighbours, and finally strangers (Form and Nosow, 1958).

COMMUNAL RELATIONS	EXCHANGE RELATIONS
Analogous to kin altruism	Analogous to reciprocal altruism
Targets are kin, partners and close friends	Targets are acquaintances, strangers, business relations
Merge costs	Distinguish costs
Track others' needs	Track others' costs
Respond to others' needs	Respond to debts incurred
Immediate repayment decreases liking	Immediate repayment increases liking
Mediated by empathy	Mediated by distress (negative state relief model)
Sense of responsibility	Sense of obligation
Norm of social responsibility	Norm of reciprocity

SOMETHING TO TRY

Ask people to do a 'thought experiment'. Ask them to name in order three people to whom they might be prepared to donate a kidney if it could save their life. Do they name relatives, friends or public figures? If they nominate relatives, note whether the people they name are younger than themselves. (Although a grandparent and a grand-child share one quarter of each other's genes, altruism should be expressed more by the old toward the young because the young have their entire reproductive life ahead of them.)

Exchange relationships

There are two variants of exchange theory in regard to altruism, both involving the calculation of rewards and costs for particular courses of action. The **minimax** approach suggests that people in general try to maximize their rewards and minimize their costs. Hence the decision to offer help depends upon finding that the rewards of giving blood (sense of moral well-being) are greater than the rewards of failing to do so (time and effort available for a more enjoyable activity), and that the costs of giving blood (discomfort) are less than the costs of not doing so (guilt). Here the focus is upon the individual making implicit calculations about what is most beneficial to him or her.

In a second (and slightly less cynical) version of exchange theory, the focus is upon **equity** between individuals. A state of equity exists when the ratio of each partner's rewards and costs are the same. Note this is not to say that they behave equally altruistically to one another. Rather, what each person gets out of the transaction is roughly equal to what they put in. If a friend of yours makes the running in your friendship (arranging outings, phoning up, paying for trips), they also have the higher cost. In return, they expect to get a lot back. Perhaps you are a very popular and attractive person, so their reward is the social status they gain by association with you. Although the inputs are imbalanced, so are the rewards and in this case equity exists.

Clark (1984) performed a simple and ingenious experiment to demonstrate that people in exchange relationships are more careful to keep track of each member's input into a joint task than they are in a communal relationship. She used a popular pastime where the player has to circle words in a large matrix of letters. Two individuals had to work together on the task and could choose to use the same coloured pen (which would obscure their individual input) or different coloured pens (which would allow them to keep track of who had circled the most words). Some of the participants (all of whom were men) were led to believe that their partner (a physically attractive confederate of the experimenter) was a recently arrived, single woman, who wanted to make friends. This was designed to suggest the possibility of a close relationship developing between them. In another condition, the men were told that their partner was a married woman who lived far away from the university, so the participants believed that this would be an exchange relationship. In this latter condition, the men were significantly more likely to choose a different coloured pen than in the condition where they expected to form an enduring relationship with the woman. The point of separating the inputs was to allow the participants to keep track of their inputs, and so to know how much obligation they had incurred towards, or created in, the other person.

A POSSIBLE PROJECT

See if you get the same results as Clark did. Photocopy a word puzzle and ask people in pairs to fill it in as fast as possible. Some pairs should be relatives (a mother and child, or a brother and sister) and others should be people who do not know each other. Offer them a handful of pens to choose from.

Another study examined how paying back a favour affected the relationship. In this study, male participants expecting either a communal or exchange relationship helped a woman with a task for which points were awarded. Some of the men then received a note from the woman simply thanking them for their help. Others received a thank-you note, and, in addition, one of the points she had earned. In the exchange condition, the men liked the woman more when she repaid their help with a point, but in the communal condition, they liked her less. Other studies showed that in exchange relationships, we like another person less when they ask for favours from us, but, if they have previously done us a favour and we are able to repay them, we like the other person more.

It seems that in casual interactions with others, we do respond as if we expected equity. Inequity results in less warm relations. This idea is reflected in the **norm of reciprocity**. Anthropologist Alvin Gouldner has pointed out that this general rule – an expectation that people will help and not harm those who have helped them – appears universally in all human cultures. As a social norm it becomes a behavioural expectation, and the dynamics of conformity come into play. People who violate this norm can expect to be rejected by others if they are detected

SAQ
6

What does equity mean, and how is it different from equality?

Communal relationships

Communal relationships are those we have with family, romantic partners and close friends. We are inter-dependent – our well-being is closely bound up with theirs. In these relationships, solidarity and harmony are emphasized, and when a task has been successfully competed, rewards are allocated on the basis of equality (everyone receives the same) rather than on equity (everyone receives a share proportionate to their contribution to the task). Where another person's need is great, even equality is abandoned, and people will give the other person all of the benefits of a joint task. In such relationships we pay attention not to the other's inputs (what they have done for us) but to their needs.

It has been suggested that humans regard pets as part of the family. Is our treatment of them more in line with kin altruism or with reciprocal altruism?

Clark, Mills and Corcoran (1989) put participants into a waiting room alone and told them one of two things: either that a friend was performing a task in the next room, or that a stranger was performing a task in the next room. They were informed that a light would change in their room from time to time. In one condition they were told that this meant that the other person needed help (even though there was nothing the participant could do to assist them). In another condition they were told that the light meant that the other person had just made a substantial contribution to a joint task for which there would be a joint reward. The experimenters simply measured the number of times that the participants looked up at the light (even though the light never changed through the course of the ten-minute study). As expected, friends looked at the light far more in the need condition than did strangers, and strangers looked at the light more in the input condition than did friends.

Communal altruism may be linked to another norm – the **norm of social responsibility**, which states that we should help those who are dependent on us. This norm encourages us to go beyond family and friends and to help others whom we do not know. When we donate money to charity, we do it because of others' need, not so that we can benefit from that charity at a later date. However, it seems that this norm is more unquestioningly applied to kin and friends than to strangers. We would more readily risk our lives to save our child or our partner than a stranger. When it comes to helping strangers, this norm seems to be qualified by a clause which adds 'Help those in need unless their misfortune has been created by their own actions'. This qualified norm involves making *attributions* about the causes of the other's need. In one study, students received a phone call from a student they did not know who said he was in their lecture class and needed to borrow their notes to help him get through an upcoming exam. In one condition the student explained that his poor notes were not his fault, but in the other he said, ' I just don't seem to take good notes in there … sometimes I just don't feel like it, so most of the

Figure 2.3: Charitable activities

notes I have are not good to study with'. Not surprisingly, other students were much less likely to help him if they believed he simply couldn't be bothered to take his own notes. When AIDS charities first began their work, their primary obstacle was people's belief that homosexuals and drug addicts deserved their fate. People were far more sympathetic when it was revealed that AIDS could be passed through blood transfusion and heterosexual intercourse, towards which there was much less stigma attached.

In summary, helping one another has been good for our species and an evolutionary argument does not mean that we are naturally selfish. Relationships depend upon give-and-take, though we seem to help relatives and close friends more naturally than we help strangers. All societies value altruism, and this is reflected in norms which promote and sustain it.

3 Altruism and Emotions

So far we have talked about acts of altruism as they form part of relationships between people. But many psychologists have been interested in how moods and emotions in our own minds might affect our willingness to help others.

Empathy and distress

Perhaps empathy is the feeling that prompts us to help others. **Empathy** means identifying and 'feeling with' another person. (Sympathy is a very similar concept but carries connotations of being on one someone's side. We can empathize with our enemies though we may not sympathize much!) In children, empathy is positively associated with prosocial behaviour and negatively associated with aggression. Women are more empathic than men. But how does empathy arise? How do we experience at second hand the feelings of another person? Although one-day-old infants cry when they hear another infant crying, we suspect that this is caused not by empathy but by distress at the unpleasant noise.

As developmental psychologist Jean Piaget has documented, infants and young children are primarily **egocentric** – by which he means not that they are selfish, but that they are unable to imagine how the world seems to another person. Real empathy probably does not emerge until toddlerhood, when children develop a **theory of mind**. Imagine you watch someone walking out of a shop. After a few steps they stop and check their pockets, turn round and retrace their steps, scanning their eyes back and forth over the ground and finally go back into the shop. Effortlessly you realize that the person has lost something and is looking for it. 'Theory of mind' refers to the way in which children engage in desire–belief reasoning. From a given piece of behaviour (searching), they impute desire (the individual *wants* to find something) and belief (he *believes* that he dropped it or left it inside the shop). Without such an ability, other people's actions would appear strange and inexplicable.

Figure 3.1: Children helping
each other

Without it, we would not be able to experience another's distress and know how to end it.

A POSSIBLE PROJECT

The 'Smarties test' is often used to assess whether a child has achieved a theory of mind. Children are usually able to pass this test at about four years of age so try it out (with their parents' permission) on children between the ages of two and five years of age. Without the child seeing you do this, take a Smartie box, or other sweet box, empty out the contents, fill it with crayons and replace the lid. Now show the box to the child and ask him or her what they think is inside. They will hopefully say 'Sweets'. Then open the lid, show them the real contents and say what they are ('Oh look, it's crayons'). Now tell them, 'In a minute I am going to show it to another boy or girl. What do you think they will say when I ask them what is inside?'. If a child has a theory of mind, they will be aware that the next child does not possess the knowledge that they have just acquired, and so the next child will think there are sweets inside. If the child does not have a theory of mind, they will be unaware that others' minds are different from their own and they will answer 'Crayons'. Whatever the child's answer, be sure to give them a smile and perhaps some sweets too as a reward for helping!

Batson has argued that empathy prompts altruism. In a subtle but important distinction, Cialdini has argued that it is distress, not altruism, that triggers helping and he calls this the **negative state relief model**. Batson believes that empathy motivates us to help another person independent of our own psychological state, whereas Cialdini believes that we only help another person in order to reduce the unpleasant distress that we are feeling (see Box 3.1).

Batson and his colleagues conducted a study in which participants saw a woman receiving electric shocks which she found upsetting, not because they were especially painful, but because she had had a bad experience with electricity as a child. The participants then filled out a questionnaire which measured both distress (ratings of alarm, fear, shock) and empathy (compassion, concern, warmth). They then divided the participants according to whether they displayed more empathy or more distress. Half of each group was told that they would watch her take more shocks. The other half of each group was told they would not be seeing the remainder of the experiment. All the participants were then asked if they wanted to change places with the victim and take the shocks for her. The predictions for the four groups were clear. Distress is a highly aversive state of personal discomfort, but it can be terminated by leaving the scene. With empathy, there should be a continuing sense of concern because one knows that the victim's suffering has not ended. Batson found that altruism was lowest amongst predominantly distressed subjects who were leaving the scene. It was higher in all other groups, but there was little difference among empathic subjects as a function of whether they were going to stay or leave (Batson, O'Quinn, Fultz, Vanderplaz and Isen, 1983).

Why did staying or leaving make a difference to distressed but not to empathic participants in their levels of altruism?

In response, Cialdini and his associates had their participants watch a victim experiencing electric shocks after being instructed to empathize with the victim. Half of the participants were then given praise or money to relieve their negative mood. These participants were less likely to offer to take the shocks

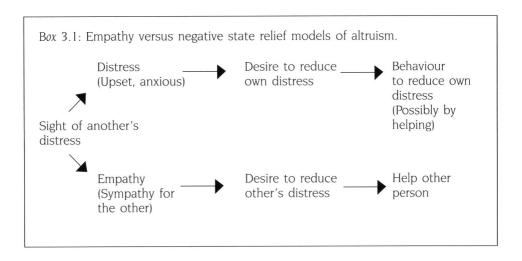

Box 3.1: Empathy versus negative state relief models of altruism.

Distress (Upset, anxious) → Desire to reduce own distress → Behaviour to reduce own distress (Possibly by helping)

Sight of another's distress

Empathy (Sympathy for the other) → Desire to reduce other's distress → Help other person

on behalf of the victim than were the participants who had not had their bad moods artificially improved. They concluded that it was the participants' mood state, not their empathy, that prompted helping (Manucia, Baumann and Cialdini, 1984).

Batson then argued that, if Cialdini was correct, empathic participants should not help if they believe that their mood state will improve regardless of whether they help or not. In his next experiment, participants again were exposed to a needy victim who appealed for help. Before they could offer to help (or not), some were told that they would be shown a film that would improve their mood. Batson found that participants helped the victim regardless of whether they believed they would have their mood improved or not (Batson, Batson, Griffitt, Barrientos, Brandt, Sprengelmeyer and Bayly, 1989).

The issue is not yet resolved but here is one suggestion. Batson (1991) notes that selfless and self-serving motives may both be at work. But he argues that we are more likely to feel empathy when we feel a close attachment to the person who is suffering. It may be that empathy-based altruism is involved in communal relations and has arisen from kin altruism. If it is, then we would expect empathy to be greatest between those who care about each other deeply or among people who view their relationships in communal terms. Distress-based empathy may be more likely where we have no intimate or long-term relationship with a sufferer, and can terminate our own distress *either* by helping *or* by leaving the scene. Our choice may be decided by the rewards and costs that apply to the two options.

Some films' emotional impact depends upon eliciting empathy from the audience. The tragic endings of Love Story, Terms of Endearment, *and* West Side Story *seem to be particularly aimed at women. Can you think of films aimed at men which aim to elicit empathy with the hero's plight? Are they different in their characters and plot?*

SOMETHING TO TRY

Next time you see a newspaper advertisement for a charity which uses a heart-rending picture to capture your attention, try to examine your own reactions. Do you turn the page to relieve your distress or does your empathy with the people in the picture haunt you for hours afterwards?

The effects of prior mood

We have already seen that Trivers believes that emotions are related to reciprocal altruism because they act as cues to our credits and debts in an exchange relationship. Social psychologists have also been interested in moods but examine their role in predisposing people to act generously rather than in regulating the state of their relationship. A consistent finding is that good moods are associated with generosity and altruism. When subjects are told that they have done well on a creativity test, they donate more to charity than when they are told they have done badly.

However it seems that good moods only prompt altruism when it involves *helping*, rather than hindering, another person. After receiving (or not receiving) free biscuits while they were studying in the library, students were asked if they would volunteer to assist by acting as a confederate in a psychology experiment. In one condition they were told that they would have to help a participant with a task while in another they were told that their role would be to interfere with a participant's performance. Those who had been put into a good mood by the biscuits volunteered more but only if they could help, rather than obstruct, a participant. This has been taken to mean that we try to maintain good moods and avoid activities that might vanquish them. On the other hand, it could mean that when we receive acts of altruism from others we feel generally indebted and this prompts us to help (but not hinder) others.

Why should helping be associated with a positive mood state? Evolutionary theory would suggest that acts of altruism have been rewarded in the long term by reproductive success but also in the short term by feelings of pleasure. This pleasure may result from the feeling that one is socially 'in credit', and thus has some insurance against an unknown but potentially hazardous future. Evolutionary psychologists have used a game called 'Prisoner's Dilemma' to examine whether co-operation or competition is a better strategy. In this game the two players are told that they have both been arrested for a suspected robbery. Imagine you are a player and the police say to you:

If you confess and your partner does not, you will get off with a three-month sentence (for assisting us) and your partner will go to jail for 20 years. If you both confess, you both get 10 years. If you both keep silent, then we won't be able to convict you

---

Box 3.2: Here is Thomas Sutcliffe writing in the *Independent* newspaper (March 13, 1997) about the pleasures of giving on Red Nose day.

Surely the whole point of charity is the absence of calculation — reason not the need, you know, and certainly don't do sums about what your profit will be once all the costs have come in... The only proper donative position, it seems, is head bowed, with a stone in each shoe... Aren't the celebrities just in it for their own careers, people ask, and shouldn't schoolchildren be doing something a little more self-sacrificing than going to school in their favourite clothes? Should we really be enjoying ourselves for other people's benefit? As it happens one of the guiding principles of Comic Relief has always been that of 'fair exchange' — the BBC offers airtime and resources but gets an audience-grabbing array of stars for what amounts to a bargain price; comedians give up their time but benefit from honorary membership of the Good Blokes Club; viewers and participants cough up the cash but get a top-up of glee in return... Remote poverty offers much besides — a refreshed sense of your own blessings, an opportunity for sincere connection, even a moral example of courage — all precious commodities. Indeed, perhaps we should hope that the objects of our charity never catch on to just how good a deal it is — otherwise they might put the price up.

both for this crime but we can trump up some charge that will lock you both up for one year. Make up your mind quickly. I am making the same offer to your partner.

What are you going to do? Although in the short term the best strategy is to betray your partner, when the game is played over and over (as it is when friends do favours for one another in real life) the strategy that emerges as most successful is **Tit-for-Tat**. On any opening move, co-operate with your partner and after this do whatever your partner does. How might natural selection predispose us to such a strategy? One way is to have helping behaviour as the automatic option and to have it associated with positive feelings. We generally try to co-operate or to assist when we encounter others and only discontinue this strategy when we see that the other is not reciprocating.

We can approach the issue from the opposite perspective also. What do people in bad moods do? Children were asked to think about neutral, pleasant or unpleasant memories in order to change their mood state. They were then (1) allowed to help themselves to sweets; and (2) given 25 pence with the chance to donate some of it to charity. Children in bad and good moods took more sweets than those in neutral moods. But the most generosity to charity was exhibited by those children who were happy. This study suggests that bad moods are associated with self-centredness and lack of attention to others. Depressed individuals shun social companionship, seem trapped within themselves and incapable of understanding or caring about the distress they are causing to others around them. In Trivers' terms, they show little interest in initiating a co-operative relationship and seem to have a general pessimism about others' intentions.

One negative mood state that is associated with helping others is guilt. When participants are made to feel guilty about accidentally upsetting some computer cards, they were more likely to offer to do a favour for the experimenter. People going into a Catholic church to make a confession gave more to charity than they did on the way out (when they had had their guilt relieved by absolution). Again, Trivers can offer an explanation for this. Guilt is a state of indebtedness and it is unpleasant. We can escape this aversive mood by correcting the social balance through a generous act.

SAQ 8

Which of these three moods is not associated with increased altruism – a good mood, a bad mood, a guilty mood?

Box 3.3: Prisoner's Dilemma

		Prisoner 2	
		Co-operate (Refuse to confess)	Defect (Confess)
Co-operate (Refuse to confess)		**1 year for P1** **1 year for P2**	**20 Years for P1** **3 months for P2**
Prisoner 1			
Defect (Confess)		**3 months for P1** **20 years for P2**	**10 years for P1** **10 years for P2**

Collecting money for a registered charity is a worthwhile thing to do. It also allows you to watch how people respond to your presence and to see which people are most likely to make a donation. If you can persuade a friend to work with you, why not make yourself distinctively different from one another and take turns collecting? One might look like an impoverished student, the other like a business executive. Or try positioning yourself in different places — do people give more on their way into a pub than on their way into a supermarket?

Costs of being helped: Status and help-seeking

Receiving help from another puts you in a position of temporary indebtedness and this may entail a loss of status. Flood victims who have been only slightly affected by the disaster are looked upon as inadequate for seeking help. People who are particularly sensitive to their status are less likely to ask for help than are others. It is a well-known observation that men, but not women, would rather drive for hours round an unknown town than ask a stranger for help! When men and women were able to choose which opposite sex person they wanted to help them, men chose an unattractive woman whereas women chose an attractive male. When men need help they are reluctant to lose status in the eyes of an attractive woman and prefer to do it in the eyes of an unattractive one (Nadler, Shapiro and Ben-Itzhak, 1982).

Box 3.4: Is psychopathy a cheating strategy?

Linda Mealey (1995) has suggested that we can understand psychopaths as individuals who pursue a cheating strategy in their interactions with others. They manipulate, exploit and accept beneficial acts from others while never repaying them. Psychopaths are characterized by irresponsible and unreliable behaviour. They are unable to form lasting relationships and though they have a superficial charm, they lack the social emotions of love, shame, guilt, empathy and remorse. It is this deficit which makes them particularly good at cold-heartedly exploiting others. Guilt is what usually motivates us to increase our prosocial behaviour and to put ourselves back in social credit after drawing on others' help, but psychopaths rarely feel this emotion. They can appreciate that they have caused distress to another person (their intelligence is normal and they are skilled manipulators) but they do not empathize with another person and so cannot appreciate their suffering.

As we have seen, the most successful long-term relationships are based upon tit-for-tat. Psychopaths, however, seem to lack the emotions which predispose us to co-operate and help others. They behave selfishly, as if they will never meet their partner again. Now provided they are right about this, they can get away with their selfishness, for they will not encounter the same sucker twice. This is especially likely to be true in densely populated areas like cities, where people's past reputation does not precede them and every stranger is a potential sucker. However it is only a successful strategy if a few people use it; if too many psychopaths are about, they cannot successfully con each other. Psychopathy is a frequency-dependent strategy — it can survive as long as not too many people use it. About three to four per cent of the male population, and one per cent of the female population, are psychopaths.

In other studies using same-sex helpers, it was found that both sexes preferred to receive help from an unattractive person, possibly because attractive people are presumed to be socially superior to others. High self-esteem participants are less likely to ask for help and especially avoid asking for help from other people who are very like them. Participants who were asked to perform a difficult cognitive task on the computer were told that if they got stuck they could get help from the experimenter's assistant or from the computer. Participants preferred to get 'secret' help from the computer (Karabenick and Knapp, 1988), perhaps because they wanted to avoid public loss of status.

SAQ 9

Why do people with high self-esteem avoid asking for help?

Costs of helping: Bystander apathy

In 1966, the killing of Kitty Genovese in New York prompted psychologists to ask why people are so reluctant to help in an emergency. Kitty Genovese was stalked and then repeatedly stabbed by her killer for over an hour. On two occasions the killer was disturbed by bedroom lights coming on as 38 people heard the sound of screams and looked out into the night. Nobody called the police or intervened until it was too late. The third attack led to Kitty Genovese's death.

This phenomenon has come to be called *bystander apathy*. Latané and Darley (1968) conducted a series of studies to examine it. In one typical study, participants were seated in cubicles connected by an intercom for a discussion. They were told that they were with one, two or four other participants. One of the participants then explained that he or she suffered from epilepsy. As the discussion continued, this participant started to become incoherent and cried for help – obviously having a seizure. When participants believed they were the only one present apart from the victim, 85 per cent of them went to offer help. But if they believed there was another participant present, only 62 per cent did so and where they thought that there were four others, only 31 per cent did so. The presence of others clearly stopped individuals from offering help. But why? After examining about 50 studies of this effect, Darley and Latané believe that three processes are at work: social influence on interpretation; audience inhibition; and **diffusion of responsibility**.

Interpretation

When the situation is ambiguous and we are not sure if it is a true emergency or not, we often look to others for information on what is going on. If others seem indifferent to the event, we conclude that it cannot be a real emergency. For example, when groups of individuals heard a man fall and then cry out in pain all of them went to help, but when they heard the fall but no cry far fewer did so. How we interpret the situation may go beyond merely how much injury has occurred. In one study, participants witnessed a physical fight between a man and a woman. In some cases, the woman shouted, 'Get away from me. I don't know you', while in another she said, 'Get away from me. I don't know why I ever married you'. Bystanders intervened 65 per cent of the time in the first condition, but only on 19 per cent of occasions in the second.

Audience inhibition

People strive to behave in accordance with the group norm and they infer the norm from others' behaviour. If others fail to help, they fear group disapproval for helping, and, conversely, if others help (implying a normative approval of such action) they also rush to assist. Neighbourhood Watch Programmes are a way of assuring members of a community that their intervention in a crime will meet with local approval rather than censure. Censure may take the form of believing that the help-giver is a busybody or trying to impress others with their courage.

Diffusion of responsibility

Blame for failure to help can be equally shared by all members of a group; if there are four other people present, you only have to take 20 per cent of the blame, while when we are alone we must shoulder the full 100 per cent of responsibility. This effect can be overcome by identifying particular people as having special responsibility. In one study, people on a beach were asked by a researcher if they would guard his portable radio while he took a swim. When a 'thief' stole the radio, 95 per cent of those asked to guard it actually pursued the thief along the beach . When not especially asked to look after it, only 20 per cent of those who witnessed the event intervened. Nurses help in medical crises even when others are present, possibly because their training makes them feel especially responsible for giving assistance.

Intervention then seems to depend upon three questions that we ask ourselves. Is this really an emergency? Will I look foolish if I rush to assist? Isn't there someone else who can help instead of me? All three questions may be bound up with one another. Imagine forcing the door to enter a neighbour's house because you are convinced there is a violent episode occurring when in fact it is simply a raucous game of charades. Helping where no emergency exists may make you feel foolish, nosy or conspicuous, but it is a small price to pay for possibly saving someone's life.

SAQ 10

Give three reasons why we fail to help in possible emergencies.

4 Instrumental Theories of Aggression

KEY AIMS: By the end of Part 4 you will:
➢ *see that instrumental theories focus upon the positive material, social and interpersonal consequences of aggression;*
➢ *understand the evolutionary basis of males' preoccupation with competition and status;*
➢ *know that aggression is affected by how we encode social information, by our standards for behaviour and by our social competencies.*

There are many theories of aggression but they can be usefully split into two kinds: **instrumental** and **expressive.** Instrumental theories view aggression as serving a useful function for the individual – aggressive behaviour gains some kind of pay-off which makes it worth the risk. Aggression occurs not for the pleasure of lashing out, but for the purpose of achieving some benefit. Expressive theories (which we shall examine in Part 5) view aggression as a way of expressing and discharging anger or stress. Both types of theory find a parallel in animal behaviour and may reflect different evolutionary pathways.

Evolutionary functions of instrumental aggression

Darwin was interested in sexual selection as well as natural selection. **Sexual selection** means differences in reproductive success between individuals which affect the number of genes that an individual leaves behind in the gene pool. The most successful individuals leave behind the most offspring and the most genes. There are some important differences between men and women in how successful they can be.

In most (but not all) species, females make a greater **parental investment** than do males. In women ovulation takes 28 days. If conception occurs, a woman commits nine months of her valuable fertile life to a pregnancy, and, in prehistoric times, probably breast-fed the infant for about four years. Males, at a minimum, need only contribute sperm which is cheap and quick to produce. If a man stayed with a woman in a **monogamous** relationship, the number of children he could produce was limited by her slow rate of reproduction – he could produce only one child every four years. But men who were **polygynous** instead of monogamous impregnated many females, and left behind more children than their rivals. Because some men monopolized more than their fair

Figure 4.1: Male primate aggression.

share of women, other men were left with none and so faced 'reproductive death'. This made competition between men intense.

Among long-living social species such as primates, dominance hierarchies are a useful way to regulate aggression. A **dominance hierarchy** is a ladder of transitive relationships that indicate the relative status of members of the group. Where they exist, most aggressive encounters take place between males who are adjacent to one another in the hierarchy so that a general free-for-all is avoided. The benefits of a dominant position include first access to food and females as well as a less stressed lifestyle.

Do these insights from other species illuminate human aggressive behaviour? Martin Daly and Margo Wilson (1988) have studied homicide from an evolutionary viewpoint. Same-sex non-relative assault and homicide is far more common amongst males than amongst females in all cultures and at all historical periods that they studied. Furthermore, it peaks in the late adolescent and early adult years because this is the time when reputations and reproduction opportunities are most evident. Daly and Wilson believe that males at this age are preoccupied with issues of status and resources which they can use to subdue other males and impress females.

Are there dangers in drawing comparisons between other primates and humans? Why might human behaviour resemble that of other primates? Does similarity mean that there must be a common genetic basis for the behaviour?

Other psychologists believe that younger boys' rough-and-tumble play is a form of practice for later competitive interchanges. Interviewing 13- to 16-year-olds about their experiences, Michael Boulton (1994) found that boys more often than girls engaged in playful fighting; thought it was important to win a play fight; thought they could tell who was the strongest person in a play fight; believed that as they had grown older their play fighting had become rougher; thought that it was important to be good at real fighting; and wanted to be the best fighter in their class. Boys' dominance hierarchies have been found in most cultures (from African hunter-gatherer societies to Switzerland) and emerge at about six years of age. Dominant boys tend to be tough, attractive, strong, with good athletic ability and earlier sexual maturity. A dominant position is also very long-lasting; a boy's position at age six predicts his dominance ten years later.

In contemporary society, high-status males are rarely those that are the physically strongest. Politicians are elected and millionaires established on the basis of their intelligence, ambition and leadership, not the size of their muscles. Remember that evolutionary theory is not concerned with what is useful for us today but what was useful for us thousands of years ago. In hunter-gatherer societies, young men who were brave, strong and fearless may have been preferred by women and so had a significant advantage in leaving their genes behind. Little boys who practised fighting when they were young may have grown into the most respected positions when they were older. Any evolutionary legacy that we have is also affected by the learning environment of the individual, which is what we will now look at.

SAQ
11

Do dominance hierarchies increase or decrease aggression?

Social learning theory

B.F. Skinner argued that all learning occurs because of the consequences that follow an act. We tend to repeat acts the results of which act as a **reinforcement**. *Positive* reinforcement is the presentation of a desirable outcome (food, money, status), while *negative* reinforcement is the removal of an aversive stimulus (cessation of pain, hunger, discomfort). According to this view, we learn by a process of trial-and-error, unconsciously repeating those acts that lead to good outcomes.

Albert Bandura was a learning theorist who broke with this purely behaviourist tradition and argued that humans (and other animals) are also capable of no-trial learning. He presented evidence that we can acquire new behaviours simply by observing the behaviour of others. He called this process **modelling**, or learning by imitation. He also argued that we remember the outcomes of the behaviour that we witnessed, and called this **vicarious reinforcement**. Children could acquire aggressive behaviour, like any other behaviour, simply by observing others.

He demonstrated this in a classic study often called the 'Bobo doll experiment' (Bandura, 1965). Children watched a film of an adult being physically and verbally aggressive towards an inflatable bounce-back clown called Bobo. In one condition the adult model was punished for this behaviour, in another they were praised for it, and in a third condition there were no consequences shown. Children who saw the adult model punished performed a smaller variety of imitative acts than the children in the other two groups when they had the opportunity to play in the same way as the model. After this, all the children were offered rewards for each modelled behaviour they could accurately copy. All the groups did equally well. This study shows how children's tendency to imitate depends very much upon vicarious reinforcement and punishment. It

Figure 4.2: Bobo doll experiment. Courtesy of Albert Bandura, Stanford University. Reprinted in Cole and Cole, *The Development of Children*. The top row shows an adult behaving aggressively toward a 'Bobo' doll. In the two lower rows, youngsters imitate her aggressive behaviour.

also draws attention to an important distinction which Bandura made between *acquisition* (learning a new behaviour), and *performance* (spontaneously enacting a behaviour we have learned). Learning depends upon attention and memory, but whether or not we enact a learned behaviour depends upon our competence at the behaviour and upon the reinforcement we anticipate as a result of the vicarious reinforcement that we saw the model receive.

 SOMETHING TO TRY

Prime-time television viewing occurs between 8 p.m. and 10 p.m. at night. Watch some of the programmes that are shown then, with a pad and paper at hand. Note down every act of aggression, which character performs it, and to whom, and what happens to that character subsequently. Is aggression performed more by men or by women? Is it mostly done by heroes or by villains? Who are the victims? Are there rewards for the violence?

What are the payoffs for aggression?

Outside the laboratory, there are no experimenters handing out sweets for aggressive behaviour. But if Bandura is right, there must be rewards of some kind. What are they?

Material or extrinsic rewards

In some cases, there is a clear material reward for aggression. Studies of children show that in the pre-school years most acts of aggression are about taking possession, or defending ownership, of a toy. When the number of toys in a playroom is reduced, the amount of aggression among children increases. Adult violence can also get tangible rewards. Robbery, for example, is an act of violence which produces monetary pay-off. Rape is the threat or use of force to obtain sexual gratification. Hitmen commit murder not because of extreme anger but because they are paid handsomely to do it.

Reputation

More often the rewards are psychological. Richard Felson has proposed an **impression management theory** of aggression. According to this view, the pay-off for aggression is establishing or maintaining a reputation as someone who must be treated with respect. In most social situations, people strive to create favourable identities and the participants co-operate with one another in this mutual 'facework'. Politeness and tact are instances of this kind of co-operation where the actors agree to assist one another in their performance and so create a positive image of themselves for the audience. The absence of this politeness is interpreted as an offence and the victim finds himself 'altercast' in an unfavourable identity. Co-operative facework now breaks down and to avoid accepting this loss of face, the victim may counter-attack in order to discredit his opponent's identity. So begins an escalating cycle of insult and attack.

Violent criminals are especially preoccupied with issues of dominance and control over others. Felson and Steadman (1983) analysed 159 incidents of homicide and assault and found that each step in the encounter depended on the previous one in a predictable way:

(1) identity attack – insult, accusation, or pushing;

Box 4.1: Anthropologist Robin Fox was interested in impression management and aggression in his study of a small island off the west coast of Ireland. Here is his description of how honour was saved without too much injury at a local dance, thanks to the intervention of the community.

When a man makes a challenge he puts his pride on the line. He cannot back down without suffering a wounding hurt to his pride and a loss of reputation. It is an old story, perhaps older than history. It seems to tap something deep in men, to do with the old interplay of dominance and virility that we see so effectively at work in nature... Wee Johnny was out there drinking with his cronies and as the door opened a flood of light from both ends of the hall hit the dark roadway. Paddy swinging wildly at Wee Johnny caught him by surprise and grazed his mouth. As both men were more than a little drunk it is unlikely that either of them could have focused well enough on the other to make an accurate hit; but Paddy's glancing blow enraged Johnny who roared and made for his assailant. He was grabbed and held back by several hands. By now both men were rather dazed. For a while they just looked at one another – each firmly held by his supporters – and presently began shouting insults again. Over and over Paddy repeated – my translation of the Gaelic is very rough – 'You don't need to hold me, I wouldn't dirty my hands with him...' There was a last flurry; again the principals were pulled back; and now someone was bringing Wee Johnny's weeping mother forward; the crowd parted for the old lady. With prayers and admonitions she pleaded with Wee Johnny to come home and not disgrace her like this in front of friends and neighbours. Saints were liberally invoked and the Blessed Virgin Mary implored often. People hung their heads. Johnny, looking dazed, told her to quiet herself – she didn't – and hurled himself at Paddy and his group: 'I'd have yer blood if me mother hadn't come. Ye can thank her that you're not in pieces in the road, ye scum'.

(Fox, 1977, p.140-142)

(2) influence attempt – request or command to do or to refrain from doing something;

(3) non-compliance – refusal to comply with command;

(4) third party instigation or mediation – others attempt to urge one party on or to reconcile the participants;

(5) threat- verbal or gestural:

(6) evasive action – apologize, attempt to flee;

(7) physical attack – with or without weapon.

This emphasis upon public status links to the evolutionary importance of dominance and reputation.

Justice

Donald Black (1983) has argued that the pay-off for violence may be the informal restoration of justice amongst those who have no access to the courts. Imagine you have been deeply wronged by another member of the community but, as in some remote societies, there is no police force you can

Box 4.2: Wife abuse is often about issues of power and control. Men seem particularly prone to abuse when they sense that their wife is unfaithful or seeking to have an independence that will give her freedom from their surveillance. Here is one woman's story of her husband's behaviour when she went back to college to train for a job.

First he'd play cat and mouse with me. For two or three hours he'd watch me as though he were daring me to do something wrong. I'd creep around cold inside with fear. If I sat and watched TV and the chair squeaked I'd look up quickly thinking that might be the thing that would start him. Then I'd look back at the TV so he wouldn't know I was afraid. He might get mad just because I flinched. Sometimes when he hit me I'd try to defend myself. It made things worse. If I ran out of the house, Mickey would lock the door with a bolt so I couldn't get back in. I'd have to stay out there freezing or sitting in my car for an hour or so. When he calmed down he'd unlock the door. Then, if I was lucky, we could go quietly to bed. In the morning my face would be all puffy and purple. I'd put on makeup and go to school hoping no one would notice.

(McNulty and Hughes, 1980, p.164)

contact. Or perhaps you cannot call the police because you are wanted for a criminal offence or were wronged in the course of a criminal act (ripped off by a drug dealer or had your wallet stolen by a prostitute). Perhaps you live in a bad neighbourhood and the police do not take seriously crimes which are committed there. In these circumstances, vigilante violence may be common and may be considered an acceptable way of restoring equity.

Remember that in many societies some forms of violence are tolerated because the victim is believed to deserve it. Until a hundred years ago, a man could beat his wife provided that the implement he used was no wider than his thumb (hence the expression 'The Rule of Thumb'). Only in the last decade has it been an offence for a man to rape his wife. Today we allow parents to hit their children (though that may soon change). In Italy in the past it was not a criminal offence for a man to kill his wife if he found her in bed with another man.

Power and control

Some writers have argued that the benefits of aggression reside in controlling others. When we want others to do what we want, we have a variety of techniques of social influence that we can use. These include persuasion, manipulation and the use of various kinds of authority (used by parents, police, teachers and so on). When all else fails, there is coercion and physical violence. These work by instilling fear and giving the user power over the other person. Power can buy many benefits in terms of having one's needs met. Violence is a good way of getting one's meals cooked on time or getting to watch the television channel that you choose.

Norm conformity

Among some sectors of society, the use of violence may be normative and even expected. These are called **subcultures of violence**, though some have suggested that they should be renamed 'subcultures of masculinity' since it is men who are principally involved. When people are living under stressful

Figure 4.3: Gang members in New York.

conditions of poverty, anger often erupts into aggression. The more frequently anger is expressed in this way, the more 'normal' it becomes, and people's inhibitions about this kind of behaviour grow weaker. Soon aggression becomes a normative way of resolving conflict. This manifests itself in hitting children, slapping spouses and fighting with neighbours. Failure to respond to provocation with violence is taken to be 'unmanly', and, in an effort to behave appropriately, men learn to respond to insult with physical aggression because to act otherwise would (paradoxically) be considered deviant. In short, violence is expected and if someone fails to react to an insult in this way, he would have to offer some excuse or justification for his failure to do so.

SAQ
12

What is the difference between positive and negative reinforcement?

Cognitive social learning theory

Walter Mischel (1993) developed social learning theory by incorporating cognitive processes more fully. This formulation was called *cognitive social learning theory*. He described a number of factors which are crucial to the performance of a learned behaviour.

1. Encoding. How do you interpret and understand the situation you are in and the behaviour of others? Was that last remark about you a joke at your expense or a playful way of drawing you into the conversation? Is that stranger staring at you because they are hostile or because they think they recognize you from somewhere?

2. Expectancies. Often these take the form of an 'if...then' anticipation of likely events. If you assume the stranger is hostile and decide to go ahead and challenge them ('Who do you think you are staring at?'), then will the other person back down? If it turns into a fight, are you likely to win or lose? If you give them a friendly wave, will they smile back and stop staring?

3. Subjective values. What is important to you in this situation? How much do you value the peer approval you will get from your friends if you challenge the stranger? Is it important to you to be seen by others as tough and independent? Or is it important to you to show that you can manage the situation without resorting to violence?

4. Self-regulatory systems. In addition to praise and rewards from other people, individuals also have their own standards of behaviour. Self-regulatory systems mean that we are not entirely at the mercy of situations because we can generate and pursue our own goals, even in the face of others' condemnation. If we believe that aggression is never justified, then we will desist from fighting even if our friends are egging us on. Afterwards we react to our own performance with self-criticism ('Stupid of me to care what others think of me'), or with self-satisfaction ('I really managed to control my temper for a change').

5. Competencies. Competence includes our knowledge of social rules and norms and the interpersonal skills that are at our disposal in 'pulling off' an effective performance. Individuals differ in their ability to transform and use social information to create novel solutions to social problems. One problem might be that if you don't challenge the stranger, your friends will think you are scared. Some individuals are skilful in redefining situations in their favour ('I've got my new shirt on and I don't want it spattered with his blood') or redefining others' actions ('Only sad people look for fights').

SOMETHING TO TRY

Imagine that you have told a very personal secret to a friend. You later find out that they have spread the secret to all your acquaintances. Try to think of five possible things that you could do to deal with your anger and remedy the situation.

Hostile attributional bias

Kenneth Dodge (1986) and his colleagues have investigated the encoding part of this model. They surmised that highly aggressive boys may interpret the acts of others as being more hostile than normal boys do – they have a **hostile attribution bias**. To find out, they read a story to a group of boys and asked them what they thought was going on and what they would do next.

Imagine that you are standing on the playground playing catch with several other boys. A boy is holding the ball. You turn your head in the other direction, and the next thing you realize is that the ball has hit you in the back real hard, and it hurts a lot. The other boys are laughing.

Aggressive boys were 50 per cent more likely to say that the other boy had done it on purpose than were the non-aggressive boys. They also found that among seven-year-old boys, fights most frequently occurred after bouts of rough-and-tumble play – aggressive boys seem to misread playful aggression as the real thing and react accordingly. Their poor decoding skills mean that they are over-aggressive and quickly become unpopular with their peers.

SAQ
13

What five processes does cognitive social learning theory think are important in understanding aggressive (and other) behaviour?

Reducing aggression

According to instrumental theories, there are three principle ways to reduce aggression in society.

1. Modelling effects. We must reduce children's exposure to violence, but especially to violence that meets with rewards on film and television. Such films may furnish models of aggression that can be copied by children. In Part 6, we will consider in detail the impact of the media.

2. Reducing rewards. We must ensure that aggressive behaviour does not result in rewards. For children in the home, this means paying particular attention to negative reinforcement. Highly aggressive children show a pattern of coercive exchanges with their parents in which their increasingly aggressive behaviour results in their parents' 'giving up' on discipline. In this way, their behaviour is reinforced by the termination of their parents' aversive 'nagging'. In adults, we need to find ways to make sure that aggression is not effective in achieving power, control or self-esteem. In Britain the Zero Tolerance programme (zero tolerance of domestic violence) tries to make people aware that wife-beating should never to be condoned under any circumstances. We should aim for a society where aggression is considered to be a deeply embarrassing and shameful behaviour.

3. Social information processing programmes. Aggression in childhood is predictive of violence in adulthood, hence early intervention is important. Children at primary school need help to understand that injury is not always intended, that aggression leads to a loss of friends, and that there are many ways that conflict can be handled that do not include physical attack.

Figure 4.4: Zero Tolerance campaign advertisement.

Expressive Theories of Aggression

KEY AIMS: By the end of Part 5 you will:
➤ *see that expressive theories focus upon aggression as a result of an individual's emotional state;*
➤ *be able to identify ecological factors which are associated with aggression in animals and man;*
➤ *understand the distinction between frustration, negative affect and arousal as sources of aggression.*

Expressive aggression refers to actions whose function seems to be to discharge unpleasant feelings of arousal by lashing out at the source of our anger. We shall consider how angry feelings are provoked and why they are sometimes expressed as aggression. But first it is useful to ask if animals show their own kind of expressive aggression.

Evolutionary functions of expressive aggression

Animals fight about scarce resources. We saw in Part 4 that, among males, status is one such resource because it gains sexual access to females and increases reproductive success. But for all animals, male and female, there are other, more tangible, resources at stake, such as food and safety. One way a group of animals can defend these resources is by claiming a territory in which each animal has enough space to provide for its food needs. But what happens when food becomes scarce or when the population size becomes too great?

Each species has a preferred social distance – the distance that they routinely keep between one another. Crowding signals to animals that their population is getting too big. Animals must either emigrate to new areas, or find other ways to reduce population numbers, such as by spontaneous abortion of pregnancies, cannibalism, infanticide and high levels of aggression. Animals such as humans, who produce few offspring and invest very heavily in each of them, are especially intolerant of crowding. One way of looking at human expressive aggression is as a legacy of this need to ensure spacing. Too little personal space, high temperature, discomfort, and insufficient resources are all signals of overcrowding, and humans, like other animals, find them aversive. Our first instinct may be to escape from them, but if we cannot we may respond with aggression.

Do animals respond to crowding by aggression, escape or both?

Psychoanalytic theory

Freud argued for the existence of the **libido** – an instinctive drive towards life and the reproduction of life. The libido is an inborn and essential part of the **id,** the unconscious part of our mind that is concerned with basic survival and self-gratification. The id knows nothing of the needs or wants of others and

Figure 5.1: People struggling to grab merchandise at a sale.

demands immediate gratification. During childhood, the **ego** develops and mediates between the id and the external world. In general, the ego is sufficiently strong to keep the libidinal urges of the id at bay, but when these urges become too strong, or the ego is weak, aggression erupts into behaviour. In later writing, Freud came to believe in a death instinct, **Thanatos,** which is a drive that works in opposition to the life instinct and is usually checked and controlled by the stronger libido. When the death instinct becomes too strong, it is drained off in the form of aggression toward others. Freudian theory is now largely discredited because so few of its tenets can be scientifically examined. However, Freud's legacy lives on in frustration–aggression theory and in **catharsis** (the 'draining out' of aggressive energy). We shall evaluate the dubious merits of catharsis later.

Frustration–aggression theory

The importance of **frustration** was taken up by a team of researchers at Yale University (Dollard, Doob, Miller, Mowrer and Sears, 1939). They argued that aggression was always the result of frustration, and (in their original writing) that frustration always leads to aggression. However, Neal Miller amended this second statement when it became clear that frustration can produce other non-aggressive reactions. Instead, he said that, 'Frustration produces instigations to a number of different types of responses, one of which is an instigation to some form of aggression'.

How many different emotional and behavioural reactions to frustration can you think of?

The Yale group defined frustration as interference with a goal response. Frustration occurs when we are prevented from performing an entire pre-planned behaviour

35

sequence associated with reward. Three factors affect the amount of frustration we feel, and we can illustrate these by imagining that you are hot and tired after a tennis match and are desperate for a cold drink.

1   **How strong your drive state is**. Your level of frustration will be affected by how badly you want and need that drink.

2   **The number of frustrating incidents**. You go to the first drinks machine and find it empty. You go to the next and find it switched off. You go to the next and it refuses to accept your money. By the third encounter with a machine, your frustration level is very much higher than it was at first.

3   **Whether the goal blocking is total or partial.** You will be more frustrated if you fail to get a drink at all than if you find a machine with a broken refrigeration unit that dispenses a lukewarm can.

A POSSIBLE PROJECT

Buy a small pocket-sized notebook and keep a log for one week of the time and circumstances of every occasion on which you felt angry. Ask others to do the same. What

— Continued ...

Box 5.1: Relative deprivation as frustration?

Poverty has often been seen as an important cause of crime. Increasingly, however, criminologists are finding that it is *relative*, rather than absolute, poverty that makes people unhappy. Economic frustration can be seen as the gap between actual and expected income and lifestyle. What factors contribute to this frustration?

1. A revolution of rising expectations. In a study of 84 nations, political instability and rioting increased in line with modernization. Literacy and urbanization make people aware of material goods, but because affluence spreads slowly, it creates a gap between expectations and reality and this can lead to frustration and anger. In the United States, the urban riots of the late 1960s were brought about because of the success of the earlier civil rights victories. African Americans had been led to expect that opportunities would immediately increase, but they did not and the frustration expressed itself in rioting.

2. Upward comparison. We tend to compare ourselves with others who have more than we do rather than with those who are worse off. Americans at every economic level (except the very highest) believe that they would be happier with a ten to twenty per cent increase in their income. However, upward comparison may not be good for our sense of personal satisfaction. After participants were asked to complete one of the following sentences five times, 'I'm glad I'm not....', or 'I wish I were....', those in the first condition felt more satisfied and less depressed with their life than those in the second.

3. The adaptation level phenomenon. We quickly habituate or adapt to an improvement in our living conditions. What at first seemed luxurious now seems simply necessary. (Studies in the United States show that although ownership of cars, televisions and other household appliances has increased drastically since the mid 1950s, self-rated happiness has actually decreased slightly.) Lottery winners who are first elated by their new wealth soon adjust to it as a normal state of affairs, and report no greater happiness than before they won.

... continued

percentage of the anger episodes were caused by frustration? What goals were frustrated and how? Do frustration–anger episodes occur more frequently at times of tiredness (for example, at night) and stress (for example, when there are many demands being made on you at the same time)?

There are three aspects of the frustrating experience that later studies have shown will increase or decrease aggression: how arbitrary it is; whether aggression will put an end to the frustration; and whether some account is offered to excuse the frustration.

Pastore (1952) argued that it is *illegitimate* or *arbitrary* frustration, not just frustration *per se*, that leads to anger. In the Yale group's original study they had asked people to rate their anger in response to different scenarios of frustration. For example, participants were asked how they would feel if they were waiting at a bus stop and the bus passed by without stopping. Pastore rewrote these scenarios to give an explanation for the frustrating event – the bus had 'Garage' written on the side, indicating it was not in service. Participants reported much lower levels of anger. We feel especially angered when we feel that we have been treated without due consideration.

Is frustration aggression theory able to explain why insults are a powerful cause of aggression? What (if any) goals do insults prevent us from attaining?

Buss (1966) has argued that while frustration may make us angry, it leads to aggression only when the aggression relieves or ends the frustration. That is, in his view, frustration only leads to aggression when it is *instrumental* – it achieves the goal of terminating our unpleasant mood.

When we know of circumstances that *excuse* another person's frustrating behaviour, we are less inclined to behave aggressively towards them. Participants in one study were treated very rudely by a graduate student, but then it was explained that he was studying for an exam and was under a great deal of stress. This made his behaviour more forgivable and participants gave lower levels of retaliation (see Box 5.2).

SAQ
15

Name three factors which affect frustration levels and three factors which diminish the impact of frustration on aggression.

SOMETHING TO TRY

Interview some drivers about their experiences of road rage as both victims and aggressors. Do they mention frustration? It has been suggested that the fact that we cannot communicate with the other driver increases our anger because when a driving error is made, the offender cannot offer the usual justifications and excuses. Have you noticed any signs that drivers use to make apologies or to offer thanks?

Cognitive Neo-Associationist Theory

Leonard Berkowitz (1989) revised frustration–aggression theory. His model (see Box 5.3) attempts first to explain what causes anger and then to explain how

Box 5.2: Justifications and Excuses

Imagine you were supposed to meet a friend but forgot all about it. You later phone them, hoping to avert their frustrated anger with you. You can try using justifications or excuses. A justification is an explanation in which someone accepts their responsibility for an act but denies that the act was wrong. An excuse is an explanation where someone acknowledges that an act was wrong but denies full responsibility. Here are some examples:

Justifications

Appeal to loyalty	I would have been there but my sister fell over and I had to take her to hospital.
Appeal to higher authority	I would have come but my mother wouldn't let me.
Social comparison	You have no right to be angry – you've done the same to me in the past.
Self-fulfilment	I would have come but I didn't really want to and I am trying to be more assertive toward others.
Effect misrepresented	Oh, come on, it wasn't that bad. You didn't wait long and you weren't busy anyway.

Excuses

Accident	I'm sorry, I didn't mean to forget.
Failure to foresee consequences	I didn't think you would mind.
Lack of capacity	I tried to come but the bus didn't arrive.
Lack of volition (Physical)	I was ill and I couldn't get to the phone to warn you.
Lack of volition (Psychological)	I was so exhausted/angry/depressed that I couldn't see anyone.
Amnesia/Fugue state	Date? What date?

Derived from Tedeschi and Reiss (1981).

this anger may be expressed as aggression. The starting point of his model is not frustration but negative affect (feeling bad). Frustration may be one cause of this but there are many others. Pain, for example, causes rats to attack each other and we all know the momentary and irrational feeling of anger when we stub our toe or bang our funny bone. High temperatures also make us feel bad. In a study of riots in the United States, researchers found that in 15 out of 17 cases it had been unusually hot the day before the disturbance. The same effect has been demonstrated in the laboratory, where participants are more aggressive in a 95°F (35°C) room than in a cooler environment. Bad smells,

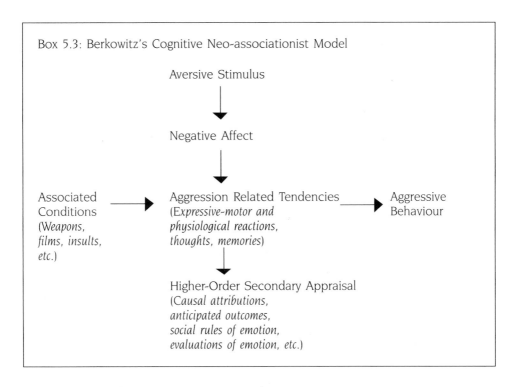

Box 5.3: Berkowitz's Cognitive Neo-associationist Model

Aversive Stimulus

Negative Affect

Associated Conditions (*Weapons, films, insults, etc.*) → Aggression Related Tendencies (*Expressive-motor and physiological reactions, thoughts, memories*) → Aggressive Behaviour

Higher-Order Secondary Appraisal (*Causal attributions, anticipated outcomes, social rules of emotion, evaluations of emotion, etc.*)

cigarette smoke and crowding have all been found to increase levels of aggression. These, and other unpleasant events including stress, frustration and insult, produce negative affect.

This generates primitive tendencies both to fight and to flee, as either one will have the effect of getting us away from the source of the unpleasantness. One of these tendencies will be more dominant and will result in rudimentary feelings of either anger or fear. These rudimentary feelings are composed of expressive-motor reactions (clenched fists), physiological changes (increased **sympathetic nervous system** activity), and the **priming** of a neural network which contains memories and images relating to anger or fear. This is an automatic and unconscious process of blind association.

There may be a secondary appraisal of the situation and of our dominant response. We consider whether anger is an appropriate emotion, and this may heighten or diminish our anger. It also leads to a more differentiated emotional experience. Rather than being simply angry, we may feel jealous or outraged or contemptuous. These cognitive appraisals can happen just after the rudimentary emotion but they can also happen later when we brood about the event. After receiving a back-handed compliment at a party, many of us will have had the experience of lying awake, trying to assess whether it was an intended insult and what the motivation was.

However, Berkowitz emphasizes that these secondary thoughts are not themselves the causes of aggression – they are accompaniments to feelings of anger. Aggression can occur as a blind rage before these higher order processes can operate. He points out that studies showing the cooling effect of justification present the mitigation before or at the time of the frustration. If there is too much of a delay, the aggression-related tendencies have already triggered aggression and the secondary thought processes (including mitigating attributions) are too late to stop it.

When aggression-related tendencies have been triggered, the likelihood of aggression occurring depends upon other situational factors. While anger 'pushes' aggression to the surface, Berkowitz believes that **cues** (objects that are associated with aggressive behaviour) can also 'pull' aggression out of mere anger. Berkowitz (1965) has shown that viewing a violent film (*Champion*, about a prize fighter) caused participants to behave more aggressively to a 'learner' on an electric shock machine than did participants who had watched a non-violent film.

Another demonstration of the role of cues to aggression has become known as the 'weapons effect' (Berkowitz and LePage, 1967). In this experiment, participants were set high shock levels by a confederate of the experimenter. They were then allowed to retaliate. They were taken into a separate room where there was a revolver and shotgun on the table or a shuttlecock and two badminton rackets or no objects other than the shock key. As predicted, the angered participants who saw the weapons gave higher shocks that did the participants in the other two conditions. However, the study has been criticized as artificial and as having strong 'demand' effects – perhaps participants were more aggressive because the expectations of the experimenter were obvious. Other researchers have failed to replicate the finding.

Arousal Transfer Theory

Berkowitz argued that aversive experiences directly and immediately produce negative affect. But Dolf Zillmann had a different idea that was stimulated by the work of Schachter and Singer (1962) on emotion. They had shown that the experience of emotion depends upon two processes: physiological **arousal** and cognitive labelling. Arousal is activation of the sympathetic nervous system – it brings with it sweating, pupil dilation, increased blood pressure, heart rate, respiration and muscle tension and it interrupts digestion (imagine how you feel on a roller coaster and you have a good idea of what the sympathetic nervous system does). These bodily changes prompt a search in the immediate environment for clues as to what has provoked these changes. We interpret them as euphoria (if we are at a great party), or terror (if we are followed on a dark street at night), or anger (if we are insulted or frustrated).

Zillmann offered a different interpretation of Berkowitz's findings. He argued that watching the film *Champion* produced a state of heightened physiological arousal in the participants. This arousal transferred to the shock-giving situation and produced a stronger experience of anger and consequent

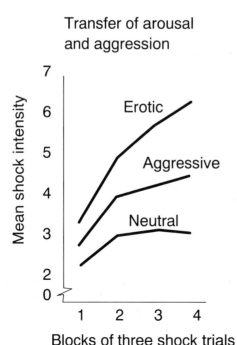

Figure 5.2: Zillmann results graph.

retaliation than the participants in the co[...]
tested this in a very ingenious way (Zillman[...]
one of three films: *Champion*, an erotic filn[...]
(measured by blood pressure) was highest in t[...]
and finally the educational film. Now Berkow[...]
in the *Champion* condition because it ha[...]
However, Zillmann predicted that the most[...]
erotic film because the participants' height[...]
in the experimental situation as anger. The[...]

What do you think Zillmann's work has to say about now viewing pornography might [...] violence?

While Berkowitz believes that negative affect comes 'ready labelled', Zillmann believes that arousal is non-specific until we have interpreted it. Arousal can be transferred from one situation to another and we can be easily fooled into mislabelling it. According to his idea, arousal left over from one activity can energize reaction in a new situation. If you have just come off the dance floor at a night club, you are more likely to respond aggressively to an insult than if you had been sitting quietly watching others dance.

To show this, Zillmann had participants ride an exercise bike to increase their arousal. He reasoned that at the point they finish exercising, their arousal is at its height but it is also clearly attributable to the exercise. If participants are given the opportunity to be aggressive at this point, then despite their high arousal they will believe correctly that it is the result of exercise and not misattribute it to anger. His data on retaliation supported this idea.

SAQ 16

Berkowitz and Zillmann agree that anger is a direct and unmediated response to an aversive stimulus. True or false?

Reducing aggression

1. Negotiation not catharsis. Recall that Freud believed that aggressive impulses were inevitable but that they could be released by expressing them in a non-injurious way – a process called *catharsis*. This suggestion has been taken up by some therapists who encourage their clients to punch cushions or scream to get rid of their anger. However, catharsis seems to increase rather than decrease subsequent aggression. Spectators at aggressive sports events (American football, wrestling and ice hockey) show more hostility when they leave than when they enter. If catharsis were effective, then we would expect that people who behave aggressively at one point in time should be less aggressive later. Studies demonstrate exactly the reverse – aggressive people remain aggressive over time.

So should we bottle up our anger? No. If something is wrong in a relationship, it will go on being wrong until it is addressed. If someone's behaviour is upsetting you, the best thing to do is to arrange a quiet time to talk privately with them. The aim is to explain your view of the situation and to ask the other person how they view it. Often they will be quite unaware of how their behaviour affects you. If the differences of opinion persist, you should jointly

Box 5.4: Does catharsis help a marriage?

The method we used to see if catharsis, or ventilation, helps couples with deep conflicts to avoid physical violence is like the method used to test conflict theory. We divided the sample of couples into four groups according to the depth of their disagreements over money, sex, children, housekeeping and social activities. We further divided each group into those who follow the advice of the ventilation school and expressed their pent-up hostilities by such things as swearing, insulting, smashing or throwing objects (but not throwing things at their partner) and doing spiteful things. These are all verbally or symbolically aggressive acts which, if the catharsis theory is right, should allow people to rid themselves of pent-up aggression before things get to the point of direct physical attack on a spouse.

In all four groups, the results showed that verbal aggression and physical aggression go hand-in-hand. In fact, the link between verbal blasts and physical blows is *greatest* for couples with the most conflicts. The irony of this is that the high conflict couples are the very ones for whom letting off steam verbally is supposed to be the greatest help in avoiding violence (Straus, Gelles and Steinmetz, 1980, p. 170).

negotiate a settlement. The main thing is to be clear about what specific changes you want ('Please don't call me "love"'), rather than vague requests ('I want more respect').

2. Explanations can mitigate unavoidable frustrations. We have seen that anger as a response to frustration can be lessened by providing explanations and showing consideration for those who are affected. Motorway roadworks are often announced in advance, explanations of what is being done (and why) can be posted and we are now all familiar with the 'Sorry for any delays' notice at the end of roadworks. These go some way to alleviating drivers' annoyance.

3. Not all frustrations can be avoided and we expect children to learn from an early age how to deal with them. Some adults, however, engage in behaviour that they would find unacceptable in their children – kicking, cursing and sulking. Frustrations are particularly hard to cope with when we are under stress, but it is important to keep a sense of perspective. Reduce your sympathetic nervous system activity by breathing slowly, clear your mind of anger and ask, 'Will any of this really matter five years from now?'.

The Impact of Culture

KEY AIMS: By the end of Part 6 you will:
➤ *know what is meant by culture;*
➤ *understand why the link between televised violence and aggression in society has been hard to demonstrate;*
➤ *see how interpretations and values affect altruism and aggression.*

What is culture?

Culture has many meanings for the person on the street and also for academics who study it. We will define **culture** as 'socially transmitted knowledge'. Culture is what is acquired from the people around us rather than by genetic predisposition (such as attachment behaviour in infants), by trial-and-error learning (such as classical and operant conditioning), or by 'off-line' thought experiments ('What if I were to...'). Socially transmitted knowledge may be:

(1) Technological. For example,how to operate a computer or track a wild animal;

(2) Social. For example, 'Did you know that Susan is going out with John?';

(3) Interpretative. For example, 'Have you got a problem?' spoken by an angry person is a challenge, not an offer to provide help;

(4) Evaluative. For example, a belief that altruism is good.

It is important to bear in mind that differences between societies can be brought about by ecological adaptation, rather than by the social transmission

Figure 6.1: Photo of children watching TV.

of knowledge. For example, the prevalence of street gangs in inner city areas of the United States may be a response to the high crime rates in these areas against which the gang may offer protection. Nonetheless, once such gangs have formed they may spread culturally – middle-class suburban youths hear about gang 'colours' and their macho reputation and take it up themselves, even though they have no need for protection from crime.

We will make a distinction between the cultural *medium* and the cultural *message*. One of the most powerful forms of cultural transmission is the medium of television, and we will begin by examining the controversial question of whether TV violence causes an increase in viewers' violence.

SAQ
17

Name four types of information that can be transmitted culturally.

The medium of social transmission

Theories of the television–violence relationship

John Hinckley was one of the many thousands of people who watched the film *Taxi Driver*, in which Robert De Niro tells Jodie Foster that he will kill a political candidate unless she returns his love. In 1981, John Hinckley attempted to assassinate the then American President Ronald Reagan and a note was found in his hotel room addressed to Jodie Foster telling her that he was going to kill the President for her. In England, the tragic killing of two-year-old Jamie Bulger was attributed by the judge to the two ten-year-old boys having watched a video in which a child is systematically tortured. What is the link between viewing and committing violence?

1. Cognitive social learning theory. Recall the classic Bobo doll study (see Section 4). Bandura demonstrated that children can learn new behaviours from watching a model, and the probability of their spontaneous enactment depends upon the reinforcement or *punishment* received by the model. This effect occurs in the real world too. A study of London executions between 1858-1921 indicated that there was a temporary drop in the murder rate in the week of the execution and this drop was affected by how much press coverage the execution received. Unfortunately, in much fictional TV violence the offender is not punished.

Cognitive social learning theory emphasizes values and this suggests that we would be less likely to imitate violence that is portrayed as *immoral* or *wrong*. In one study (Berkowitz, 1965), all participants saw an identical film of someone being beaten up. However, in the first condition they were given information suggesting that the victim had exploited and mistreated others and was getting his just desserts, while in the second he was described as a 'nice guy'. After watching the film, those in the first condition (who had been told the victim deserved his fate) gave more electric shocks to another participant. Unfortunately, in many films we are invited to view the aggression as justifiable, and even morally desirable, when it is meted out by a hero against villains.

Another important factor is how much the viewer *identifies* with the violent actor. Participants who were instructed to empathize with a boxer while viewing him on film winning a prize fight were more aggressive subsequently than participants who had not been instructed to empathize.

Finally, believing that the violence is *real* can increase imitation. A group of children viewed a film of a violent university demonstration, but some were told it was real footage, while others were told it was just actors pretending. Children who thought the action was real were more likely to be aggressive after the film.

2. Priming. According to Berkowitz's cognitive neo-associationist model, the activation of aggression-related thoughts and feelings is critical. In line with this, he argues that television violence is easily remembered because it is highly visual and dramatic. These memories prime aggressive thoughts which can lead to aggressive behaviour.

3. Aggressive scripts. For psychologists, a **script** is a mental representation of a behaviour sequence as it occurs in time. For example, we all have a restaurant script which includes being shown to a table, being given a menu, placing an order, receiving food, getting a bill, paying and leaving. Television may provide scripts for what should happen when two people disagree. (Recall from Part 4 that there is a predictable pattern of events in assault and homicide cases.) If deprived of other non-violent solutions, a diet of violent television can make people resort to the only script they know.

4. Desensitization. It may be that watching a steady diet of violence reduces our emotional reaction to it. We get used to seeing blood and pain, and the effect is an emotional blunting. In one study, participants were shown news footage of a riot. Those who had watched a piece of fictional violence on film immediately before showed less physiological arousal to the riot scenes than did those in the control group. In addition, participants who reported regularly watching violent TV in their real lives showed a weaker response to violent films.

These are some of the theories of how violent TV might induce aggression. But what is the evidence that there is a relationship between watching violent TV and aggression?

What four factors are associated with increased imitation of television violence?

Viewing television violence and behaviour

After years of research, no certain conclusions can be drawn about the impact of televized violence. In part this stems from problems with research methods. Early studies asked about children's television viewing preferences and then correlated this with their level of aggression (which was measured by self-report or by asking classmates to nominate the most aggressive children). Unfortunately these studies are not informative because a correlation does not tell us whether TV violence causes aggression, or whether aggressive children prefer to watch more violent TV programmes.

A second line of investigation has looked at the short term effects of violent TV. Experimenters expose participants to violent TV and then measure their later aggression in the laboratory, but these studies are extremely artificial; the effect upon aggression is small and inconsistent and any priming effect usually wears off within one hour. Others have conducted field studies which are nearer to real life and which look for longer term effects. In a typical study of

Box 6.1: The effects of pornography

- Pornography is a form of erotica designed to excite sexual arousal. The erotic movies which have caused most social concern are those where force or coercion is used to accomplish a sexual act.

- In many films (such as the classic *Gone with the Wind*) the woman is portrayed as initially resisting the man's attempts to seduce her but then melts in his arms. Such portrayals may play a part in allowing men to believe that 'No' does not really mean 'No'.

- Laboratory studies show that men give more electric shocks to women when they have watched a film in which a woman's initial refusal changes to sexual pleasure than after films in which a woman is depicted as distressed by having forced sex. Pornography-induced aggression is directed at women – the administration of shocks to men is unaffected by the films.

- Rapists find films of rape more arousing than depictions of mutually consenting sex. For some rapists, sexual pleasure is heightened by their control or power over the victim.

- Worldwide, as pornography became more freely available in the 1960s and 1970s, there was a rise in rape rates except in those countries and areas with laws controlling the sale and use of pornography.

- Serial rapist and murderer Ted Bundy said, 'You reach a point where the pornography only goes so far, you reach that jumping off point where you begin to wonder if maybe actually doing it would give you that which is beyond just reading it or looking at it'.

- Feminist Robin Morgan said, 'Pornography is the theory and rape the practice'.

this type (Leyens, Camino, Parker and Berkowitz, 1975), a group of adolescent boys in a Belgian correctional institution were divided in half and one group watched a nightly diet of violent TV for a week while the other half watched non-violent films. The level of aggression in the following week was then measured, showing an apparent increase in aggression in the first group. However, when we examine the measures of aggression closely, we find that they include exclamations ('Boy, am I crazy!), threats ('I'm going to get you') and yelling. As the authors themselves admit, many of these actions sound more like rough-and-tumble adolescent play than serious aggression. A meta-analysis examined the magnitude of the effects found in a number of studies such as these and concluded that they were too small to moderate (Wood, Wong and Chachere, 1991).

Longitudinal studies follow the same group over time and the biggest of these was the Columbia County Study, which tracked all the children in a small rural area from the age of nine onwards (Eron, Huesmann, Lefkowitz and Walder, 1972). They measured violent TV viewing and aggression at ages nine and 19 years. First they found that exposure to TV violence and aggression were correlated at age nine. More importantly, they then calculated the correlation between age nine viewing and age 19 aggression, *and* age nine aggression and age 19 viewing. If there is a cause-and-effect relationship, then the first correlation should be larger than the second. This is what they found.

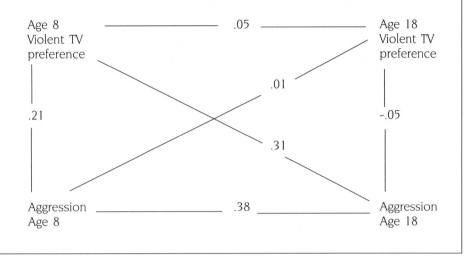

Box 6.3: Correlations between viewing violent television and aggressive behaviour at two different ages (from Eron, Huesmann, Lefkowitz and Walder, 1972).

Age 8 Violent TV preference ———— .05 ———— Age 18 Violent TV preference

.21

.01

.31

-.05

Aggression Age 8 ———— .38 ———— Aggression Age 18

However, there are problems (Durkin, 1995) . Measures of viewing habits were obtained by asking the parents, and the way that programmes were classified is open to question – Bugs Bunny was classified as violent while Donald Duck was classified as non-violent. The children's aggressiveness was measured by asking school mates to name children who were, among other things, most likely to stick their tongue out and be rude to teachers. In adulthood, aggression included number of traffic violations. These do not seem to be valid measures of aggression as it is usually defined.

It is important to remember that, while some individuals may be affected by violent TV, the vast majority of us are not. Television forms only one part of our social environment, and watching TV is not a passive activity. Our reaction to it depends upon what we bring with us – our backgrounds, interpretations and values. More research needs to establish the factors that make some people vulnerable to violent TV.

SAQ 19

A correlation between watching violent TV and aggression measured at a single point in time may mean:
(1) *viewing violence causes aggression;*
(2) *more aggressive people watch more violence on TV;*
(3) *some other factor (such as a need for excitement) causes both aggression and preference for violent TV;*
(4) *all of the above.*
Which answer do you think is correct?

The cultural message

Values

The value that we accord to acts (seeing them as morally worthy or unworthy) is an important factor in understanding the form and frequency of different behaviours. Differences between cultures in the importance they assign to the individual and to the group may relate to the values they hold about hurting or helping others. **Collectivism** means that a higher value is placed on the family, group or nation to which one belongs than on the individual members. **Individualism** means that the individual is seen as the fundamental and most valuable unit of a society. Hofstede (1980), in a survey of IBM employees in different countries, found that North American, Australian, British and Dutch employees were the most individualistic, and employees in Taiwan, Peru, Columbia and Venezuela the least. In Japanese culture, the family and the work group are accorded very much higher reverence and loyalty than they are in the West. While Westerners who seek therapy are often advised to express their emotions, Morita therapists in Japan teach their patients to suppress their emotions and to practise self-discipline.

These values can have important implications for helping others. Individualism requires a belief in, and respect for, formal processes of justice in order to regulate the relationships between selfish individuals. To examine this, Miller and Bersoff (1992) asked American and Indian participants about various moral dilemmas. In one story they were asked to imagine they were in Los Angeles (or Mysore) and had their best friend's wedding ring which had to be delivered to him in San Francisco (or Bombay) by the following day. They were told they had no money to buy a train ticket. Should they steal a ticket from another passenger? If participants said yes, they were indicating that they believed interpersonal obligations took precedence over formal justice. Thirty-nine per cent of Americans said yes, but 84 per cent of Indian participants said yes. Collectivism seems to be associated with a greater emphasis upon interpersonal obligation at the expense of formal mechanisms of justice.

How could we make predictions about aggression from the perspective of individualism and collectivism?

Interpretations

To fully understand a piece of behaviour we also have to take into account the meaning that it has for those who participate in it. Peter Marsh (Marsh, Rosser and Harre, 1978) did just this with British soccer 'hooligans'. He used the term 'aggro' to describe the unruly Saturday afternoon behaviour of fans which looks extremely aggressive, but in fact leads to surprisingly little injury. He set out first to describe why and how aggression is **ritualized** into aggro, and then to understand how fans come to talk about it in an apparently self-contradictory way.

There are distinct groupings among the fans that dictate seating arrangements at the match – *Rowdies* (aged about 15, noisy, dressed in club insignia, carrying banners); *Town Boys* (aged between 18–25, more mature, no special uniform); and *Novices* (children of about ten who spend much time watching and learning from the antics of the Rowdies). Within these groups various roles are identifiable: *Chant Leader* (initiates chants and interposes home team chants against those of the opposition); *Aggro Leader* (accepted as a 'hard man' based on his local reputation, but not required to engage in much actual fighting); *Nutter* ('crazies' whose unpredictable, unreasoned action may even involve launching physical attacks on the opposition); *Hooligans* (boys who engage in disruptive but primarily humorous acts for the amusement of other fans; and *Organizers* (responsible for coach hire, petition signing, organizing 'whip rounds', and so on).

Box 6.4: Altruism and Hutterite communities.

The Hutterites are a fundamentalist religious sect which began in sixteenth century Europe and migrated to North America in the nineteenth century to avoid conscription. Their values require complete altruism from their members. Hutterites regard nepotism and reciprocity as immoral – putting others before oneself must be without regard to kinship or to expectations of return. They practise community ownership; no private goods or property are allowed. They discourage individuality in appearance, dress or home furnishings. When a settlement becomes too large, it must split into two. This is done by drawing up two lists of members matched for age, sex and skills. The night before the split, one of the lists is drawn by lottery and this group must leave the next day to establish a new community. Personal relationships are always subordinate to the group's interests. How do the Hutterites manage to foster such a highly altruistic approach to living?

- Like the Jews they have been subject to persecution and this has encouraged a strong in-group allegiance against out-group prejudice.

- They elevate selflessness as a moral and religious virtue: 'If only we loved the life of poverty as Jesus showed it, if only we loved obedience to God as much as we love being rich and respected!'.

- Selfishness is reviled as sinful. 'The sinner lies in all of us; in fact to sin, to be selfish, is our present inclination. Left to ourselves we shall end up in damnation...'.

- They emphasize that members share the same fate. 'Life in the community presupposes that each will work for the benefit of others as much as for himself; that no-one will be egoistic. The moment this assumption is undermined, mutual suspicion, jealousy and mistrust arise'.

- They have developed procedures for regulating members who behave selfishly. A first sin will meet with 'brotherly admonition'; if this fails, the sinner will publicly face the whole community. If he fails to mend his ways, he will be sent away. Even then he may be taken back into the church if he shows genuine repentance.

However demanding such a lifestyle may be, the majority of children choose to stay with the community as adults. Where pure altruism can be culturally sustained and fostered, the group benefit, and so, at a spiritual level, do individuals.

These roles are co-ordinated around a script. Prior to the match there is chanting back and forth between the two ends of fans which sounds quite intimidating ('You're going to get your f*****g head kicked in'; 'There's going to be a nasty accident'). When the teams appear at 2:50 p.m. there is a deafening escalation of chants directed towards noteworthy players on the opposing team. At half-time as the teams change ends there may be skirmishes, 'hard looks' and threats but little actual violence among the rival fans. Finally, at the end of the game, the home team fans 'see off' their opponents by chasing them back to their bus. Marsh argued that fans understand the ritual element of aggro. They admit that much of what appears to be violence is merely noisy threat and that the aim of the encounter is to challenge the

In Parts 4 and 5 we discussed the distinctions between instrumental and expressive theories of aggression that academics have offered. In an attempt to understand how ordinary people explain their aggression, Steven Muncer and I asked men and women to talk informally in same-sex groups about their own experiences. Men seemed to talk about aggression in the language of instrumentality – they saw aggression as a way of controlling others and from that control they gained social respect and private self-esteem. Women talked about aggression using the language of expressiveness – they saw aggression as a loss of self-control which happened when they were feeling very stressed. Afterwards women report feeling guilty about their behaviour. In line with this idea, other studies have shown sex differences that support the view that men and women interpret aggression differently (Campbell, 1993). Here are two typical accounts: the first is from a woman and the second from a man.

We had a terrible fight. It probably was nothing important. I can't remember what it was about. But it did terminate with him going in and taking a shower, and I was furious! I just sort of whirled round and I tried to pick up the phone. I don't know if I wanted to throw it, but I knew it wasn't going to go far enough. So I picked up a frying pan that was right there and I tossed it right through the curtain. I didn't even think about it and then he came out dripping holding the frying pan. And he said, 'You could have killed me! You could have killed me, do you know that?' I still didn't realize I could have killed him because I didn't feel like I wanted to kill him... I could have flung it against the wall, I just threw it at him. I really have a very blind kind of rage sometimes when I seem to get really crazy.

I want that guy to know I'm going to beat him and I want him to back down. I don't want to hit him. I want that guy to be the guy to say, 'OK – we're not going to fight'. I want to maintain my self-respect. That's the kind of person I am. I just want to get one up on him and then walk away and go, 'Ha-ha'. It doesn't work that way most of the time. This is the problem. You take that one extra step – you can't walk off. It's the fear that's exciting. You're wired. Psyched. You start shaking. Adrenaline is flowing like crazy... And then you realize that people are listening. And it's kind of uplifting because you're on stage, you know? Everyone is going, 'Ooh, look at that over there!' You feel good. You feel kind of like, 'I have some power here. I have something over them.'

opposing fans and cause them to withdraw or submit without actual fighting taking place. Some of this knowledge is reflected in the chants, for example, 'We had joy, we had fun / We had Swindon on the run / But the joy didn't last / 'Cos the b******s ran too fast'.

What similarities can you see between the football fans here and the islanders studied by Robin Fox (see Part 4)?

At the same time, the fans sometimes talk as if the violence was real and the danger extreme. Marsh reconciles these two versions of events by pointing out that among young working-class men the demonstration of courage is crucial to their sense of identity. Matches provide an arena for such a demonstration, and a relief from the mundane weekdays of low-status jobs or unemployment. In order to claim fearlessness, they must stress the presence of real danger. So fans talk big while at the same time understanding the rules that govern the ritual. This is why fans sometimes make quite contradictory remarks such as:

Interviewer: *Well, what happens to the guy you've kicked?*
Fan A: *He's dead.*
Fan B: *Nah – he's alright – usually anyway.*

These interpretations form part of cultural knowledge. We all learn what events mean by being part of a social community. Understanding the interpretations that those involved give to their actions can help to make sense of what appears to be chaotic or random activity.

SAQ
20

Why did the football fans in Marsh's study try to exaggerate the danger of their aggressive encounters?

Summing up

At the start of this Unit I said that altruism and aggression required analysis at many different levels. While evolutionary psychology can point to the survival advantages of different strategies of altruism and aggression (among kin and non-kin and among in-group and out-group), what is truly unique about humans is their ability to interpret, explain and evaluate their actions and to transmit these to others through culture. The forces of evolution are as slow as gene transmission but the contagion of new ideas and values is rapid. The twenty-first century will certainly be dominated by global electronic communication. Let us fervently hope that we can both preserve the important differences between peoples and responsibly endorse universal values of altruism and non-violence.

REFERENCES

This list of references is included for the sake of completeness and for those planning further study or a project on the topics covered by this Unit. For most purposes, the books recommended in the Further Reading section will be more than adequate.

ALLEN, J. (1978). *Assault with a Deadly Weapon: The autobiography of a street criminal*. New York: McGraw Hill.

BANDURA, A. (1965). Influence of model's reinforcement contingencies on the acquisition of imitative responses. *Journal of Personality and Social Psychology*, 1, 589–595.

BATSON, C.D. (1991). *The Altruism Question: Toward a social psychological answer*. Hillsdale, NJ: Erlbaum.

BATSON, C.D., BATSON, J.G., GRIFFITT, C.A., BARRIENTOS, S., BRANDT, J.R., SPRENGELMEYER, P. and BAYLY, M.J. (1989). Negative-state relief and the empathy–altruism hypothesis. *Journal of Personality and Social Psychology*, 56, 922–933.

BATSON, C.D., O'QUINN, K., FULTZ, J., VANDERPLAS, M. and ISEN, A.M. (1983). Influence of self-reported distress and empathy on egoistic versus altruistic motivation to help. *Journal of Personality and Social Psychology*, 45, 706–718.

BEM, S.L. (1974). The measurement of psychological androgyny. *Journal of Consulting and Clinical Psychology*, 42, 153–162.

BERKOWITZ, L. (1965). Some aspects of observed aggression. *Journal of Personality and Social Psychology*, 2, 359–369.

BERKOWITZ, L. (1989). Frustration–aggression hypothesis: Examination and reformulation. *Psychological Bulletin*, 106, 59–71.

BERKOWITZ, L. and LePAGE, A. (1967). Weapons as aggressive-eliciting stimuli. *Journal of Personality and Social Psychology*, 7, 202–207.

BJORKQVIST, K., OSTERMAN, K. and LAGERSPETZ, K. (1994). Sex differences in covert aggression among adults. *Aggressive Behavior*, 20, 27–34.

BLACK, D. (1983). Crime as social control. *American Sociological Review*, 48, 34–45.

BOULTON, M. (1994). The relationship between playful and aggressive fighting in children, adolescents and young adults. In J. Archer (Ed.) *Male Violence*. London: Routledge.

BUSS, A.H. (1966). Instrumentality of aggression, feedback and frustration as determinants of physical aggression. *Journal of Personality and Social Psychology*, 3, 153–162.

BUSS, A.H. and PERRY, M. (1992). The Aggression Questionnaire. *Journal of Personality and Social Psychology*, 63, 452–459.

CAMPBELL, A. (1993). *Out of Control: Men, women and aggression*. London: Pandora.

CLARK, M.S. (1984). Record keeping in two types of relationships. *Journal of Personality and Social Psychology*, 47, 549–557.

CLARK, M.S., MILLS, J. and CORCORAN, D.M. (1989). Keeping track of needs and inputs of friends and strangers. *Personality and Social Psychology Bulletin*, 15, 533–542.

DALY, M. and WILSON, M. (1988). *Homicide*. Hawthorne, NY: Aldine de Gruyter.

DODGE, K. (1986). Social information-processing variables in the development of aggression and altruism in children. In C. Zahn-Waxler, E. Cummings and R. Iannotti (Eds) *Altruism and Aggression: Biological and Social Origins*. Cambridge: Cambridge University Press.

DOLLARD, J., MILLER, N.E., DOOB, L.W., MOWRER, O.H. and SEARS, R.R. (1939). *Frustration and Aggression*. New Haven, CT: Yale University Press.

DURKIN, K. (1995). *Developmental Social Psychology*. Oxford: Blackwell.

ERON, L.D., HUESMANN, L.R., LEFKOWITZ, M.M. and WALDER, L.O. (1972). Does television violence cause aggression? *American Psychologist*, 27, 253–263.

FEINGOLD, A. (1994). Gender differences in personality: A meta-analysis. *Psychological Bulletin*, 116, 429–456.

FELSON, R. and STEADMAN, H. (1983). Situations and processes leading to criminal violence. *Criminology*, 21, 59–74.

FORM, W. H. and NOSOW, S. (1958). *Community in Disaster*. New York: Harper.

FOX, R. (1977). The inherent rules of violence. In P. Collett (Ed.) *The Rules of Social Behaviour*. Oxford: Blackwell.

GILLIGAN, C. (1982). *In a Different Voice*. Cambridge, MA: Harvard University Press.

HOFSTEDE, G. (1980). *Culture's Consequences*. Newbury Park, CA: Sage.

KARABENICK, S.A. and KNAPP, J.R. (1988). Effects of computer privacy on help seeking. *Journal of Applied Social Psychology*, 18, 461–472.

LATANÉ B. and DARLEY, J.M. (1968). Group inhibition of bystander intervention in emergencies. *Journal of Personality and Social Psychology*, 10, 215–223.

LEYENS, J.P., CAMINO, L., PARKE, R.D. and BERKOWITZ, L. (1975). Effects of movie violence on aggression in a field setting as a function of group dominance and cohesion. *Journal of Personality and Social Psychology*, 32, 346–360.

MANUCIA, G.K., BAUMANN, D.J. and CIALDINI, R.B. (1984). Mood influences on helping: Direct effects or side effects? *Journal of Personality and Social Psychology*, 46, 357–364.

MARSH, P., ROSSER, E. and HARRE, R. (1978). *The Rules of Disorder*. London: Routledge and Kegan Paul.

McNULTY, F. and HUGHES, F. (1980). *The Burning Bed*. New York: Harcourt, Brace, Jovanovich.

MILLER, J.G. and BERSOFF, D.M. (1992). Culture and moral judgement: How are conflicts between justice and interpersonal responsibility resolved? *Journal of Personality and Social Psychology*, 62, 541–554.

MEALEY, L. (1995). The sociobiology of sociopathy: An integrated evolutionary model. *Behavioral and Brain Sciences*, 18, 523–599.

MISCHEL, W. (1993). *Introduction to Personality (5th edition)*. New York: Harcourt, Brace, Jovanovich.

NADLER, A., SHAPIRA, R. and BEN-ITZHAK, S. (1982). Good looks may help: Effects of helper's physical attractiveness and sex of helper on males' and females' help-seeking behaviour. *Journal of Personality and Social Psychology*, 42, 90–99.

OLWEUS, D. (1979). Stability of aggressive reaction patterns in males: A review. *Psychological Bulletin*, 86, 852–875.

PASTORE, N. (1952). The role of arbitrariness in the frustration–aggression hypothesis. *Journal of Abnormal and Social Psychology*, 47, 728–731.

RIDLEY, M. (1996). *The Origins of Virtue*. London: Penguin.

RUSHTON, J.P., FULKER, D.W., NEALE, M.C., NIAS, D.K.B. and EYSENCK, H.J. (1986). Altruism and aggression: The heritability of individual differences. *Journal of Personality and Social Psychology*, 50, 1192–1198.

SCHACHTER, S. and SINGER, J.E. (1962). Cognitive, social and psychological determinants of emotional state. *Psychological Review*, 69, 379–399.

SPENCE, J., HELMREICH, R. and STAPP, J. (1974). The Personality Attributes Questionnaire: A measure of sex role stereotypes and masculinity–femininity. *Journal Supplement Abstract Service Catalog of Selected Documents in Psychology*, 4, 42 (Number 617).

STRAUS, M.A., GELLES, R.J. and STEINMETZ, S.K. (1980). *Behind Closed Doors: Violence in the American family*. New York: Anchor Books.

TEDESCHI, J. and REISS, M. (1981). Verbal strategies in impression management. In C. Antaki (Ed.) *The Psychology of Ordinary Explanations of Social Behaviour*. London: Academic Press.

TRIVERS, R. (1985). *Social Evolution*. Menlo Park, CA: Benjamin Cummings.

WOOD, W., WONG, F.Y. and CHACHERE, J.G. (1991). Effects of media violence on viewers' aggression in unconstrained social interaction. *Psychological Bulletin*, 109, 371–383.

ZILLMANN, D. (1971). Excitation transfer in communication-mediated aggressive behaviour. *Journal of Experimental Social Psychology*, 7, 419–434.

FURTHER READING

BARON, R.A. and RICHARDSON, D.R. (1994). *Human Aggression, 2nd edition*. New York: Plenum.

CAMPBELL, A. (1993). *Out of Control: Men, women and aggression*. London: Pandora.

RIDLEY, M. (1996). *The Origins of Virtue*. London: Penguin

SPACAPAN, S. and OSKAMP, S. (Eds) (1984). *Helping and Being Helped:Naturalistic studies*. Newbury Park, CA: Sage.

TAVRIS, C. (1989). *Anger: The misunderstood emotion*. New York: Touchstone/Simon and Schuster.

TEDESCHI, J.T. and FELSON, R. (1995). *Aggression and Coercive Actions: A social interactionist perspective*. Washington, DC: American Psychological Association.

ANSWERS TO SELF-ASSESSMENT QUESTIONS

SAQ 1 Altruism is one form of prosocial behaviour. Other forms of prosocial behaviour have an explicit expectation of reward attached (for example, a salary).

SAQ 2 Ambition is a *drive* towards achievement. Aggression is an intentional injurious *act*. Anger is an *emotion* that may or may not lead to aggression. Hostility is a specific or general *belief* in others' ill-will.

SAQ 3 Anti-social behaviour can be examined by the use of experiments, field studies, questionnaires and criminal statistics. Autobiographies can describe what anti-social behaviour feels like from an insider's perspective.

SAQ 4 According to kin selection, identical twins should behave more altruistically towards one another. In fact they should be as concerned with the survival of their co-twin as with their own survival.

SAQ 5 Reciprocal altruism depends upon:
(1) a stable social group;
(2) a good capacity to distinguish and remember faces;
(3) good long-term memory.

SAQ 6 Equity means that the reward/cost ratio is proportionate for each member of the relationship. Equality means that each member's rewards and costs are identical.

SAQ 7 Distress is caused by the sight of someone suffering. If you can leave the scene your distress will end. If you have to stay and continue watching the victim, your likelihood of helping will be as great as that of an empathizer but for different reasons. Distressed participants help to alleviate their own distress, not the victim's.

SAQ 8 Bad moods are not associated with altruism because depressed subjects tend to focus only on themselves. Good moods and guilt are both associated with

altruism – the first because it maintains the good mood and the second because it alleviates the sense of obligation by squaring the debt.

SAQ 9 Being helped places the beneficiary in a position of temporary subordination. High self-esteem people do not like to see themselves as 'needy' because it undermines their sense of self-worth.

SAQ 10 Failure to help may be the result of:
(1) social influences on interpretation which make people fail to define the situation as an emergency;
(2) audience inhibition which makes people fear that help-giving may be normatively deviant;
(3) diffusion of responsibility which means that others who are present must shoulder some of the blame for failure to help.

SAQ 11 Dominance hierarchies, once formed, decrease overall rates of aggression because individuals 'know their place', and aggressive skirmishes are directed primarily at those in adjacent places in the hierarchy.

SAQ 12 Both kinds of reinforcement tend to increase the frequency of the antecedent behaviour. Positive reinforcement is the presentation of something pleasant (money, sweets, praise), while negative reinforcement is the removal of something unpleasant (nagging, a ban on television watching, a curfew). Negative reinforcement is not the same as punishment.

SAQ 13 Encoding, expectancies, subjective value, self-regulatory systems, competencies.

SAQ 14 Crowding increases competition for scarce resources and animals may react by a scramble strategy (flee to a new territory), or by a contest strategy (fight for your share of the resources).

SAQ 15 Frustration is increased by the strength of drive state, the number of frustrating incidents and whether the goal blocking is partial or total. The impact of frustration on aggression is diminished by the legitimacy of the frustration, the offering of justifications and excuses and in cases where aggression will not be instrumental in ending the frustration.

SAQ 16 False. Berkowitz believes anger is an immediate and direct response to an aversive stimulus, but Zillmann claims that the stimulus produces non-specific arousal which we interpret as anger depending on situational cues.

SAQ 17 Culture can transmit technological, social, interpretative and evaluative information.

SAQ 18 Television violence is more likely to be imitated if the viewer sees no punishment for it; if the violence is portrayed as morally acceptable; if the viewer identifies with the aggressor; and if the violence is thought to be real.

SAQ 19 (4) All of the above.

SAQ 20 By exaggerating the danger, it makes their actions seem more heroic and so they can lay claim to greater heroism.

GLOSSARY

Aggression: an intended injurious act which the victim is motivated to avoid.

Altruistic: acts which benefit someone else, undertaken with no expectation of reward to the actor.

Antisocial: acts which cause harm to others.

Arousal: activation of the sympathetic nervous system preparing the body for fight or flight in the face of danger. Associated with sweating, pupil dilation, increased heart rate, respiration and muscle tension.

Catharsis: Freudian idea that aggressive energy can be released or drained out by aggressive action.

Collectivism: giving priority to the goals of one's own group and defining one's identity accordingly.

Communal relations: intimate relationships based upon meeting others' needs.

Cues: objects in the environment that are associated with a behaviour and tend to elicit it.

Culture: socially transmitted knowledge.

Diffusion of responsibility: effect associated with bystander apathy where the presence of others makes an individual feel less responsible for helping.

Dominance hierarchy: a set of linear transitive relationships defining relative status among members of a social group (a 'pecking order').

Ego: Freudian concept describing the psychological processes that impose control on the id.

Egocentric: unable to imagine how events might appear to another person.

Empathy: understanding of, and compassion for, another's distress.

Equity: a state in which the rewards of a relationship are proportionate to the costs.

Exchange relations: relationships based upon keeping track of rewards and costs.

Expressive theories: theories of aggression which view aggression as the behavioural manifestation of anger or arousal.

Frustration: blocking or thwarting of a goal response.

Genes: smallest unit of hereditary transmission carried on chromosomes.

Hostile attribution bias: tendency to attribute hostile intention to socially ambiguous acts.

Id: Freudian concept describing the unconscious, primitive part of the mind that demands immediate gratification.

Impression management theory: a theoretical perspective which sees interpersonal behaviour as a form of drama in which people act out particular roles.

Individualism: giving priority to individual rather than group goals and defining one's identity accordingly.

Instrumental theories: theories which view aggression as a means of achieving social or material goals.

Kin selection: showing particular altruism to one's relatives because they carry many of the same genes as you do.

Libido: Freudian drive which is responsible for life and reproduction of life.

Minimax: a strategy of minimizing costs and maximizing rewards.

Modelling: observational learning brought about by watching a model.

Monogamous: marriage system based on commitment to a single partner.

Natural selection: process proposed by Charles Darwin describing the differential survival of members of a species which determines which genes will survive in the next generation's gene pool.

Negative state relief model: the idea that behaving altruistically can alleviate personal distress caused by watching another's suffering.

Norm of reciprocity: an expectation that people will help those who have helped them.

Norm of social responsibility: an expectation that people should help those who are in need.

Parental investment: investment of time and energy by a parent in an offspring.

Polygynous: marriage system based on men having multiple wives.

Priming: activation of a cognitive schema or set of associated thoughts.

Prosocial: actions which benefit others and have positive social consequences.

Reciprocal altruism: the idea that altruism can be the product of natural selection if one behaves altruistically to others who have the same genetic predisposition to behave altruistically also.

Reinforcement: consequences of an act that make it more likely to be repeated. Reinforcement can be positive (presentation of a reward) or negative (removal of a punisher).

Ritualized: a highly constrained (rather than spontaneous) pattern of behaviour. Among humans rituals often convey a symbolic meaning.

Script: a mental representation of a sequentially structured event such as eating in a restaurant.

Sexual selection: process proposed by Charles Darwin describing the differential reproductive success of members of a species which determines which genes will be most numerous in the next generation's gene pool.

Subculture of violence: face-to-face communities in which aggression is the expected response to conflict or challenge.

Sympathetic nervous system: one branch of the autonomic nervous system which prepares the body for fight or flight (*see* arousal).

Thanatos: Freudian drive toward death which works in opposition to the Libido.

Theory of mind: the mechanism that allows us to infer other people's beliefs and desires.

Tit-for-Tat: a strategy of co-operation or reciprocal altruism which states, 'On the first move behave altruistically. On subsequent moves do what your partner does'.

Vicarious reinforcement: reinforcement contingencies that affect the likelihood of behaviour, but are based on watching a model receive reinforcement

ACKNOWLEDGEMENTS

Figure 1.1   L. Howling, Barnaby's Picture Library.

Figure 1.2   Mike Slattery.

Box 1.1   Items from *The Aggression Questionnaire*. Reproduced by kind permission of Professor Arnold Buss.

Box 1.2   Taken from John Allen (1978) *Assault with a Deadly Weapon: The autobiography of a street criminal*. New York: McGraw Hill.

Figure 2.1   K. J. Eddy, Barnaby's Picture Library.

Figure 2.2   Mike Slattery.

Figure 2.3   G. C. Hahessy, Barnaby's Picture Library.

Figure 3.1   Reproduced by kind permission of Isis Brook.

Box 3.2   Thomas Sutcliffe, the *Independent*, 13/3/97. Reproduced by permission of the *Independent*.

Figure 4.1   Mike Slattery.

Figure 4.2   Bobo doll experiment. Reproduced by kind permission of Albert Bandura.

Figure 4.3   Author's own.

Figure 4.4   Zero Tolerance Campaign poster. Reproduced by kind permission of the Zero Tolerance Campaign.

Box 4.1   Taken from Fox, R. 'The inherent rules of violence', in P. Collett (Ed.) *The Rules of Social Behaviour*. © 1977 Blackwell Publishers. Reproduced by kind permission of the publishers.

Figure 5.1   Mike Slattery.

Box 5.2   Derived from Tedeschi and Reiss, 1981, 'Verbal strategies in impression management', from C. Antaki (Ed.) *The Psychology of Ordinary Explanations of Social Behaviour*, London: Academic Press Ltd. Reproduced by permission of the publisher.

Box 5.4   Figure by Mike Slattery.

Figure 6.1   Trevor Legate, Barnaby's Picture Library.